A Modern Guide

to

Effective K-12 Curriculum Planning

A Modern Guide

to

Effective K-12 Curriculum

Planning

FRANKLIN P. MORLEY

Parker Publishing Company, Inc.   West Nyack, N.Y.

Library of Congress Cataloging in Publication Data

Morley, Franklin P
    A modern guide to effective K-12 curriculum
planning.

    1. Curriculum planning. I.   Title.
LB1570.M68   375'.001   72-12645
ISBN 0-13-594911-4

Printed in the United States of America

DEDICATION

To my affectionate tribe:
Muriel, Bill, Gayle, Cindy,
and John.

How this book can strengthen your curriculum renewal efforts

The purpose of this book is to help educators make curriculum changes that will keep public school learning environments in a direct, vital relationship with life outside the school.

There are several ways the book may be used to accomplish this purpose. How you use it will depend upon who you are and what you are trying to do.

First, this book is a narrative about actual curriculum events. It includes an historical picture of how these events produced significant changes in learning environments for elementary and secondary students over a period of several years. Chronologically the story begins with a task force report, goes through years of deliberately designed workshops and well supported production teams, to "total-involvement" implementation with periodic revisions based on feedback from students, teachers, administrators and parents.

Second, it is an on-site evaluation of the process of curriculum renewal. Therefore, instructional leaders may wish to read it selectively, using the table of contents to identify those aspects of the process about which they want alternative ideas at this time. For instance, Chapter One treats ways of intervening in the established operation to stimulate some thought about the need for change. Chapter Two details the basic ingredients of systematic planning.

Chapter Six highlights essential supportive services and gives a detailed description of a school district's instructional planning center. And Chapter Seven focuses on the attitudes and procedures that permit a school system to be responsive to social issues, educational trends and changing technology. Thirty-five citations are given of curriculum on the move.

Finally, this book is a detailed study of practical, effective curriculum changes made in most of the subject areas of a K-12 school program. Consequently, teachers, department heads and principals may wish to use it as a primary source of data regarding who, what, where, when, why and how specific changes were made. You may also use the detailed index to locate data about the roles played by teachers, principals, students and others; eight types of workshops to accomplish specific tasks; descriptions of instructional planning in fifteen different subject areas; or any number of special topics such as "accountability," "computers and education," "feedback systems," "paraprofessionals," and "reporting to parents," to name a few.

Perhaps there is no better way to express the challenge that led to this book than to quote one sentence by Chris Argyris, Harvard psychologist, in his review of Skinner's *Beyond Freedom and Dignity*:

> Leaders of large complex organizations are striving to find new designs of organizational structures, managerial control, and leadership styles that are less mechanistic and more organic, the latter meaning that the individual has the right—indeed the responsibility—to challenge, confront, re-design, and manage the environments in which he works in such a way that the job gets done and he actualizes more aspects of himself.

F.P.M.

ACKNOWLEDGMENTS

The encouragement and assistance of many colleagues and professional associates are an important part of this book. Most significant are those of the team of superintendents, principals, coordinators, department chairmen, and teachers I have been privileged to work with in the School District of the City of Ladue. It is hoped that the descriptions of our work together will convey in part my high esteem for their professional services to youngsters and parents in our district.

I wish to extend special thanks to Mrs. Lee Werner, kind reader and expert typist of the final manuscript.

Contents

2. Applying the power of systematic planning (*Continued*)
behavioral objectives, criterion tests, and enabling activities   36

Evaluation and reporting

Later applications of systematic planning in major curriculum revision projects   40

Behavioral Objectives • Teaching Strategies • Evaluation Technique

Supporting systematic planning with flow charts and planning sheets   43

Considering the untapped resource, the student   48

Behavioral Objectives for Visual-Motor Training • Teaching Strategies • Student Goals UNIT II • Student Activities UNIT II • Introduction • Contents • UNIT I-Physical Geography Lesson A

3. Developing and coordinating curriculum planning teams . .   **63**

Attending to four functional aspects of coordination   63

Creating a functional official structure   66

Establishing over-all district goals and instituting reasonable authoritative controls over the curriculum renewal process   70

Long-range program goals for Ladue school district

Coordinating the revision of our K-12 visual arts program   74

Accountability and the processing of curriculum change   76

Utilizing shared leadership and shifting roles of students, parents, lay specialists, teachers, administrators, and coordinators   79

Legitimizing in-service work as an integral part of the regular school calendar   83

Communicating inside and outside   89

Reporting "up" and feeding "down"   90

Finding time for instructional improvement   91

4. Harvesting curriculum renewal in the classroom, the school, and the district **95**

Defining curriculum renewal   95

Authenticating all sizes and shapes of curriculum renewal   96

Asking questions to   analyze the quality of curriculum renewal   98

Executing the "active" phase of curriculum renewal in Arena One   100

Processing deliberately planned curriculum change in six months or less time   103

Initiating and supporting approved one-year and two-year text book studies with a view toward adoption   107

Designing, developing, and implementing revised or new courses over a period of one or two years   109

Researching, designing, developing, and implementing comprehensive curriculum change in a subject area over many grades and many schools   111

Describing the many-faceted three-and-a-half-year project "Innovation 68" at a suburban high school   118

Developing new diagnostic teaching skills in staff through a comprehensive K-3 research project investigating the relationship of perceptual training and learning styles   121

5. Mediating the forces of curriculum renewal **125**

Focusing on leadership   126

Recognizing the personal traits of a catalyst   126

Signaling the essential coping capacities of an educational catalyst   128

Affirming a rationale for the change process as it relates to learning, teaching, and supervising   128

Analyzing the difficulty of a group and offering specific assistance   132

5. Mediating the forces of curriculum renewal (*Continued*)

6. Creating a "friendly" environment for curriculum renewal . .   147

List of illustrations

A Modern Guide

to

Effective K-12 Curriculum Planning

ONE

Exerting a positive influence on those who plan the curriculum

One fact very clear to practitioners in the schools by the end of the sixties was that military officers, university scholars, and industrial leaders are not the best designers of curriculum for the public schools. They each have a contribution to make, yes; but it is the classroom teacher who ultimately will and does determine the character of life and learning in the classroom.

The purpose of this book, therefore, is to show how to influence the working styles of teachers and how to create conditions supportive to those working styles, so teachers and their local colleagues can make thoughtful and effective day-by-day improvement in the school curriculum.

Defining the problem

Curriculum is the never-ending invention of learning environments. It is a social process.

Learning environments consist of systems of persons, things, and activities organized to foster the developmental fulfillment and desired behavioral patterns of all learners, young and old. In a very real sense, the total community and the culture of which it

17

is a part are the pre-existing learning environment for all members of a given community.

Public classrooms are formally-organized learning environments assigned the task of teaching certain publically identified concepts, skills, and attitudes to all members of a given society. A curriculum is invented to help public classrooms accomplish their assigned task.

The inventors of curriculum who have the final and most significant effect in shaping learning environments are those persons operating in the classroom arena itself, namely, the teacher and the students.

Other inventors operate somewhat remote to the classroom and have only indirect impact on the climate and substance of the actual learning environment, at least in the case of the traditional classroom. Such remote inventors are parents, principals, central office personnel, and outside lay or professional resource people. The inventions of these persons determine the social structures, customs, technology, and goals of the larger learning arena (school, community, nation, and world). In both forceful and subtle ways these structures, customs, technology, and goals precondition why, what, how, and when curriculum inventions can occur in the classroom.

If you, I, or anyone else wishes to improve the school curriculum, it is my belief that we do so by improving the invention process of those persons involved in organizing and operating learning environments. In fact, *I would define curriculum planning as primarily the process of influencing the working style of those who invent learning environments.* Second, *curriculum planning is a process of influencing the conditions under which those inventors work.*

The primary aspect of curriculum planning is emphasized in the early sections of this book. The latter aspect is given gradually-increasing attention as the book progresses.

Acknowledging a few sticky dilemmas

We face a variety of dilemmas when we attempt to conquer the problem of curriculum improvement. I feel our orientation to the task is incomplete unless we acknowledge a few of these at the outset.

A crucial dilemma is our shortage of scientific knowledge about how to make people more inventive. This dilemma is compounded by the fact that this inventiveness is to be applied in an institutional setting.

Several additional dilemmas stem from the fact that schools are social systems within social systems.

First, there is the dilemma of legal authority. It comes in all shapes and sizes. Many administrative decisions regarding time, place, placement of students, staffing, and financial support are all fixed within the boundaries set by a system of state law. Regional accrediting associations also throw in their constraints.

Second is the question of unpredictability. Many instructional decisions have to be made without a sound prediction of what their ultimate impact will be.

Next, there is the puzzle of transitory responsiveness. One is seldom sure of the enduring effect of any cause inserted into a social situation. It would appear that principles of social engineering set the limits to which school systems are subject to influence and control. Social systems have to be nudged into new configurations. The change agent makes a well-directed nudge; sits back to see the changed response of the system, if any; then makes another appropriate nudge calculated to move the response of the system closer to a more functional configuration. The process has some similarities to the shaping of individual behavior through successive approximations.

Another is the dilemma of conflicting roles. All school district employees, from top to bottom, who come in contact with students, carry both administrative and instructional responsibilities. The proportional mix of the two roles varies from position to position. In other words, there is an administrative component in every instructional act and some instructional effect in every administrative decision.

Finally, there is the very mixed bag of individual and group morale. The cohesiveness and efficiency of social systems are directly dependent upon communication and commitment. You can expect much trouble in systems where commitment is low and communication poor. One of the major theses of this book is that the involvement of as many persons as possible in the construction of curricular plans is the most effective way to create the communication and commitment necessary for significant improvement of instructional programs.

So much for the larger picture. Let us look at operating systems.

Challenging the administration and the teachers—a flashback

Sometimes you must make a delicate incision that gradually exposes the whole complicated system. With the passage of several years, it has become apparent to my colleagues and me that the most significant incision that has occurred over the past decade in our district was the simple query: What are the realities of learning?

What reads like an innocuous, academic question led our staff down a long workshop path toward a new perspective of the educative process. That new perspective continues to grow and assert itself in our total operation today.

In the summer of 1964, as one immediate outcome of the Superintendent's Task Force Report (see Chapter Three, p. 70), this instructional coordinator set up two workshops carrying the title, "Realities of Learning."

The first was run for one week in June by the consultant, the late Dr. Donald Snygg. Seven principals, one counselor, and thirty-one K-12 teachers heard Dr. Snygg cite these realities of learning:

Nothing is so useless as an answer for which we have no question.

Meaning comes in terms of concepts you already have.

Theories evolve out of and within one's own experience.

Behavior results from the phenomenal field at the instant of action.

Learning, a change in behavior, results from a change in the phenomenal field.

Change is in the direction of greater differentiation of figures (goals) in the field related to the ideas and feelings of the learner.

Aid and direct the goal-setting of the learner.

Open doors; confront them with problems and provide them with opportunities to test out new perceptions.

Our most important and enduring goal is to discover and preserve the phenomenal self—our own picture of ourself!

The second one-week workshop on "Realities of Learning" was conducted in August that same summer by consultant Dr. Robert DeHaan. Three principals and forty-nine K-12 teachers participated with Dr. DeHaan in pursuit of the following agenda on the "Realities of Learning":

Monday—Three families of theories of learning, the behaviorists, the perceptual, and the social.
Tuesday—Applications of theories to the teaching situation, with particular emphasis on stating objectives in functional terms such that attainment of objectives is visible.
Wednesday—The development of criterion tests by which teachers can ascertain whether students have attained objectives stated in functional terms. Also, a discussion of programmed instruction.
Thursday—Teaching creativity to children, including viewing films of children in Madison Mathematics Project.
Friday—The social context of learning, including research on the "hidden curriculum" in high school controlled by the student subculture.

This workshop introduced our staff to two books which continue to be among the most basic in our curriculum planning today. These were *Preparing Objectives for Programmed Instruction* (now *Preparing Instructional Objectives*) by Robert Mager and *Taxonomy of Educational Objectives* by Benjamin Bloom, a book published in 1956, which seemed quite incomprehensible to practitioners until Mager's clever clarification of behavioral objectives.

Perhaps I can use an agricultural metaphor to help you grasp the importance of what happened in the summer and fall of 1964. With the workshops, we had plowed some ground in the minds of many staff members. These were members of the several social systems we wanted to influence. The next operation was a "seeding down" of attitudes, skills, and concepts about curriculum building which in time would bring forth a harvest of improved learning environments for youngsters in our schools.

It was crucial that all staff be involved in this "seeding down" phase if the envisioned harvest was to be lush and widespread. Let me report how this total involvement occurred over the next year and a half.

Permit me one aside comment. Some individuals and small groups realized a rewarding harvest from the early seedings a long time before the seeding had been completed throughout the system.

Seeding down necessary attitudes, skills, and concepts about curriculum making

In September, the enthusiasm of the principals who attended one or both of the summer workshops on "Realities of Learning" was sufficient to precipitate the appointment of a subcommittee of the Administrative Council to consider additional in-service on the same theme. A one-page report of this subcommittee meeting in October contained the following suggestions:

1. That a special workshop session be held for the administrative group. . . . The area of classroom testing and evaluation plus the designing, conducting, writing, and interpreting educational research would be treated in this session. . . . Its main purpose would be *to make the administrative members more competent in serving in the role of resource persons as well as leaders in building groups devoted to these same topics* during the second phase of our recommended program which follows.

I underscored that statement which proved to be one of several effective procedures, unique in our long pursuit of the realities of learning. The successful procedure was: First, train the administrative group as a cadre to assume leadership in the training of their own building staffs. As the report went on to say:

2. The first involvement of the entire staff would be a readiness phase. Under the guidance of the principal . . . building staff groups would be instructed in the rationale for setting up lesson objectives and designing criterion tests by which to measure pupil achievement toward these objectives . . . etc. .

In November, with the special help of Robert Cleary, Educational Testing Service, the administrator's subcommittee distributed a written report of its revised plans. In the second half of that memo, I briefly described for the principals what has come to be known by some evaluators as the "golden triangle."[1] From this point on, this triangle became the main frame of reference, a useful invention, for our extended work in curriculum development and systematic instructional planning. The second half of the memo read as follows:

2. The above in-service program for administrators might well be scheduled for all teachers when the administrators feel ready to handle some of the leadership roles required for such an operation. Mr. Cleary believes that we would make real progress toward an *understanding of* and *use of* the "golden triangle":

Objectives

Learning   Evaluation
Activities   Techniques

Some evaluators conceptualize this "golden triangle" as the building block of all curriculum development. To some extent, each vertex of the triangle can be used as an entrance for devising the rest of the block. However, objectives stated in behavioral terms seem most powerful in generating the related learning activities and evaluation techniques. For this reason, Mr. Cleary recommends that we proceed as we are. The terminal behavior of increased competence in the writing of classroom tests will be a very useable skill for our staff in their day-to-day operation as well as in their occasional participation in curriculum development.

The Administrative Council approved the projected in-service program at its next regular meeting. Special note should be taken of the fact that through the action of the Administrative Council,

---

[1] This model is essentially the same one as presented by Furst, E. J. in *Constructing Evaluation Instruments,* 1958, Text Ed., McKay.

the curriculum coordinator had secured authority for and commitment to a prescribed staff development program which each administrator was then obligated to implement with his staff, he being their instructional leader.

It is my opinion that use of this primary administrative "line" structure for staff development and instructional improvement works better than creating a separate supervisory division competing for the time and allegiance of the teacher. However, it does mean that instructional central office personnel need to learn how to work *as associates with* superintendents, principals, and department chairmen toward curricular change and instructional improvement. This is no easy maneuver. Chapter Three contains my most recent thinking about how it can be done effectively.

Working with the elementary staff

The approved in-service program worked as follows: First, I conducted training sessions with the elementary principals and they in turn repeated these sessions in their own buildings with their own staffs.

There were three phases of the training.

Phase I. All participants will read the programmed text, *Preparing Objectives for Programmed Instruction* by Mager, and write one sample objective in behavioral terms and a criterion test for checking out the extent the objective is achieved by the learners. A critique of these written objectives and criterion tests will be held, using the overhead projector for examining the work of the participants.

Phase II. All participants are asked to begin studying the text, *Taxonomy of Educational Objectives, Handbook I:* Cognitive Domain, by Benjamin S. Bloom, and write a series of objectives which treat a given portion of content at two or more levels of cognition as described by Bloom. A critique of these written objectives is then held.

Phase III. All participants shall engage in a 3-hour ETS workshop on how to construct classroom tests.

I wish there were some audio-visual way I might share with you some of the dynamics generated when I worked with the elementary principals. All of us were so ingrained with the "pedagese" of ambiguous, global goals of education that writing objectives in behavioral terms was like starting all over again in the business of education. When I projected their first attempts on the wall for all to see, each principal was a sitting duck for the rest of the group. And our principals are not famous for being kind to each other even in normal discussion situations.

As mentor of the operation, I gently probed with such questions as: Does your objective say what you intend the learner to be able to do after instruction? How will the learner demonstrate to you that he has achieved the objective? Will that criterion performance demonstrate what you specified in your objective, or does it require something different and thereby is inconsistent with your objective? Believe me, there was an uneasy mix of irritation and frustration in our council.

However, despite the icy stares and awkward silences, it became very clear to me that we had achieved a crucial step. Or stated as a process guideline: *a breakthrough to the strong valuing and skillful use of behavioral objectives had to occur with that administrative group before any significant change of a similar nature could occur in the rank and file of the teachers.*

Our projected in-service program was too ambitious to be accomplished as scheduled. By the end of the 1964-65 school year most of the ten elementary staffs had completed Phases I and II under the leadership of their principals. Few, if any, had done much with Phase III; i.e., the writing of test items and the constructing of test instruments. At the same time, let it be said that a few of the most motivated and talented teachers soon excelled the principals and me in the application of these new insights and skills in improving instructional planning.

Working with secondary staff

At the secondary level the story was entirely different. Little progress had been made during that first year. It was not until the Pre-session Week, August 31-September 3, 1965, that I had the time and place to involve the secondary teachers in this matter of behavioral objectives. Careful and extensive plans were laid, including an 80-page workshop booklet with worksheets and background material for each participant.

Three and a half days of Pre-session Week were scheduled for the secondary staff to write and critique their own behavioral objectives and criterion tests. Four consultants, Dr. Pitts and Dr. Bushell of Webster College, Dr. Hudgins of Washington University, and Mr. Robert Cleary of ETS assisted our staff in running this workshop. A script for my session, "Translating Course Objectives into Behavioral Objectives and Criterion Tests," reminded me that I used a set of twelve transparencies, two overhead projectors, one 12-foot screen, and a portable mike in order to engage the staff in work exercises. The text of the basic transparency I employed at that time is reproduced in Figure 1-1. It was our version of the "golden triangle."

Figure 1-1.   System of Instructional Planning Expressed in Terms of Student Performance

Describe what you intend the student to be able to do after instruction.

OBJECTIVE

*LEARNING
SITUATION*

Describe the conditions for learning that you intend to provide to enable the student to do what you specify in your objective.

*CRITERION
TEST*

Describe the kinds of evidence that you will collect under certain conditions which you will accept as demonstrating that the student has achieved the objective.

During that Pre-session Week, there were eight hours of pre-planned "input" sessions consisting of the following: Viewing of the film, *The Miracle Worker*; "The Miracle Worker and the

Behavioristic Theory of Learning'' presented by Dr. Carl Pitts and Dr. Donald Bushell; ''Translating Course Objectives into Behavioral Objectives and Criterion Tests'' presented by Dr. Frank Morley; and ''How to Construct Classroom Tests'' presented by Mr. Robert Cleary.

There were seven hours of scheduled departmental work sessions out of which I ultimately received completed report forms specifying behavioral objectives, criterion tests, and test items for selected courses in each department.

If this whole effort looks too mechanical and shallow to you, don't feel lonely. Many of our staff felt that way about this systematic approach to instructional planning. One can usually assume that instructional leaders must cope with conflict as a natural condition for curriculum rebirth. As a bit of realia here let me insert the irate, concluding remarks of a three-page typewritten letter from one of our top-flight English teachers.

> Further bemusements:
> 1. Why are public school teachers invariably talked to as if they had no education, even training? If we are so stupid, unsophisticated, unprofessional, should the education of our nation's young be entrusted to us? Or is it really merely house-breaking that is to be our objective?
> 2. What has happened to the criticism of the multiple choice test: that it tests recall, guessing (see Mager, p. 49) and penalizes the knowledgeable student who is foolish enough to think through each of the choices?
> 3. Why do we never have workshops that stimulate courage to continue practicing an art, the product of which is necessarily fluid, non-terminal, nebulous?

My way of trying to maintain a good relationship with that teacher was to respond with a four-page handwritten memo, in which I acknowledged the possible validity of her criticism and solicited her cooperation in testing out whether there were good or bad effects on students' interest and productivity when systematic planning was applied.

The ''seeding down'' and cultivation of instructional planning skills for the secondary staff continued through the remainder of the 1965-66 school year. We conducted one more total staff workshop in February. A brief description of that spectacular follows below.

Nudging further with the realities of learning

My final, demonstrative effort in the "seeding down" process was a two-day workshop for the total staff focused on the conditions of learning as per the eight types of learning described by Robert Gagnè in his book, *The Conditions of Learning*. Reprints of Gagnè's article, "The Learning of Concepts," in the *School Review*, Autumn 1965, were distributed to the staff prior to this workshop. The purpose of the workshop was to focus on the "enabling learning activities" of the ETS "golden triangle."

In retrospect, I shudder at the brazenness of my attack. I started with a humorous filmstrip using disarming baby pictures and captions commenting on the day-by-day business of teaching. Then I projected a contrived dialogue between Coordinates and Ladutes about scientifically designed instruction.

I then pointed out that in this workshop we would concentrate on what Gagnè called the external events of instruction; i.e., the activities implemented by the teacher to enable the student to acquire some improved "capacity and disposition."

If I had concentrated on "the external events of instruction," I would have been all right; but I didn't. Stepping into the role of a psychologist, I started with Gagnè's analysis of eight types of learning and was immediately in trouble; deep, "overextended" trouble.

In retrospect, I would judge that my approach was sound for a semester's course by a psychologist, but for a three-hour lecture by a curriculum specialist, it was inappropriate and ineffective. Gagnè's book on the hierarchy of eight types of learning and his discourse on the conditions to foster each is a sound conceptualization, but it needs the right person under the right conditions to get it across. Obviously, I was neither Dr. Gagnè nor a protege of Dr. Gagnè.

When using *The Conditions of Learning* for in-service, I now recommend focusing on the latter chapters. Devote the workshop time to the three major parts of the instructional complex, namely, control of the stimulus situation, refinement of verbal communications for directing the learner's effort, and control over the feedback to the learner from the events of learning. I believe such an approach would be more manageable by local instructional leaders and more comprehendible by workshop participants. The final chapters in Gagnè's book give particularly useful advice regarding the use of different media and modes of instruction to aid the learner.

Despite the inappropriate emphasis and inept performance as indicated above, it can be honestly reported that some enduring values did accrue to the staff and me from this two-day effort. The following germinal ideas were sown:

1. The teacher is the manager of the conditions of learning.
2. A seemingly simple instructional task is composed of many requisite subtasks, all of which must be properly performed if the student is to achieve the criterion test.
3. In his analysis of a student's failure to learn, the instructor must be able to identify all the subtasks involved and to determine at what point or points failure occurred.
4. Correction of student failure will come from improving the conditions of learning at the point of student failure—of course, proper motivation is the first condition.
5. Effective instructional planning requires (1) that the teacher anticipate the complex set of subtasks which the learner must master to achieve each instructional objective and (2) that the teacher arrange the conditions of learning that will enable the learner to do each subtask.
6. The objective of the management of learning is to ensure that learning will be efficient, that is, that the greatest change in the student's behavior will occur in the shortest period of time.

Harvesting up systematic instructional planning

The first harvest was the immediate feedback from staff. As is typical, our teachers were not hesitant about expressing their acceptance or rejection of both the Pre-session and the February workshops. Our formal evaluation sheets showed a very positive behavioral response of all groups to the concepts and skills dealt with in the workshops. Evidently, the great majority were trying to use behavioral objectives regardless of their over-all rating of the work sessions. Also, the great majority felt they understood objectives as defined by Mager and felt reasonably comfortable in using such objectives in their instructional planning.

In the week following the Pre-session, I issued an invitation to all secondary staff to participate in a "trial test of a system of instructional planning expressed in terms of student performance."

Twenty teachers submitted lesson plans and test instruments in response to this invitation. The interest and cooperation of department chairmen varied from one subject area to another. It would appear from a review of the central office files that the curriculum coordinator carried this project pretty much on his own through direct conferences with participating individuals and groups.

One exception was the case of social studies at the high school. The social studies chairman headed a team of three teachers who were in the second year of their development of a TV World History course, using our newly installed closed-circuit system. In each lesson plan produced by this TV team, skill objectives were listed and coded according to Bloom's taxonomy of cognitive skills.

By the end of the 1965-66 school year, this team had produced the first "packaged curriculum" of our school district. The package included a student text of forty readings, about forty TV presentations, a set of teacher lesson plans designed for each reading and/or class activity, plus end-of-unit tests related to the prescribed content and skill objectives. A 1970 summer team did a complete up-dating of this entire program.

Making a critique of instructional objectives

A general statement of criteria for making a critique of instructional objectives was issued November 1965 as follows:

To:　　Staff Members Involved in "Instructional Planning Study," Principals, Central Office Administrators

From:　Frank Morley

Re: Criteria Used by Frank Morley in Making Critique of In-
        structional Objectives (and Tests) Developed by Partici-
        pants in Study.

The criterion questions focus on three aspects of the written objectives, namely, (a) form, (b) content, and (c) significance.

Re: *Form of written objectives* (Is it in an operational form, à
la Mager?)

1. Have you described the performance you intend the student
to be able to accomplish after instruction? (What *residue* of changed
capacity or of changed attitude would you expect to find immediately
following instruction; or better, a week following instruction?)

2. Have you described the kinds of evidence that you will collect
under certain conditions which you will *accept* as demonstrating that
the student has achieved the objective? (Do you know what you'll
be looking for to tell you that a student has benefited from instruction?)

Re: *Content of written objectives* (What is included in *your
specifications* of the intended student performance?)

1. Have you described the *kinds of data* (facts, phenomena, etc.)
the student is to deal with? And have you indicated whether during
instruction he is to recall these data (''prerequisites'' to learning),
or are they to be given to him?

2. Have you described the equipment, references, or other *aids*
which are to be available to him during instruction and which he
is expected to be able to use (prerequisite skills)?

3. Have you described what the student *is to do with the given
data*, using the available tools and/or resources? (Is it clear to you
what cognitive skills and personal-social skills you are asking him
to exercise? Is it clear to you what manipulative skills you are asking
him to apply?)

4. Have you indicated any standard by which you will judge the
acceptability of his performance?

Re: *Significance of the written objective* (What value will this
achieved objective have for the student?)

1. What important cognitive, personal-social, and manipulative
(motor) skills does the objective *require* that the student exercise?
Does your professional judgment and that of other authorities identify
these skills as *generally essential* to the development of continuing
scholars and competent adults? (This is its general significance.)

2. In view of your *specific terminal behavior* for a student in your

course, how does this performance (in the objective) relate to previous and subsequent performances essential to achieving the desired, terminal behavior? Is the performance of little consequence, or only slightly or not at all useful or related to subsequent tasks leading to the desired, terminal behavior? (This is its specific significance.)

Reporting progress throughout the system

Early in the fall of 1965, the curriculum office had indicated it would periodically distribute follow-up reports of staff projects making successful applications of systematic instructional planning. At this point, I should like to present a brief summary of the "First Report of 1965-66 Instructional Planning Study." The guideline being demonstrated is that persons in official leadership roles must visibly recognize staff performances which that leadership wishes to cultivate throughout the system.

From: Jr. High School Studies Teacher
Re: Behavioral objectives put to the test.

In light of new instructional objectives presented and developed during the Pre-session meetings of [our] School District held in September, 1965, [the] Junior High librarian and I have recently completed a project combining social studies and library research skills.

In order that our junior high students might experience success and satisfaction in using the resources of the school library, we devised a plan. Through joint planning and construction of behavioral objectives (according to Mager) the librarian and I were able to introduce one hundred ninth grade, regular track students to the fundamentals of reference work.

Presented here are statements of objectives and procedures excerpted from that report:

DAY ONE

Objective: "Students should locate and list as many *kinds* of reference material pertaining to their assigned topics as they find available in the library."
Procedure: Students were given a thorough orientation to the refer-

ence section of the library. . . . They were then instructed to work in teams of three and four to locate as many materials as possible pertaining to their topic, and prepare a group list of the various materials they discovered.

DAY TWO

Objective: "Students should be able to interpret charts and graphs, comprehend reference tables, analyze maps, recognize the value of the table of contents and index, and distinguish between different reference sources, in order to complete practical exercises for independent research."

Procedure: Students were given individual self-testing, study skills materials published by Educational Development Laboratories (EDL). . . .

DAY THREE

As two-thirds of the class continued with the EDL program, the other third was instructed in the third phase of the program.

Objective: "Students should be able to locate specific answers to questions by using social studies reference books."

Procedure: Students were given two handouts prepared by the librarian. . . .

DAY FOUR

As two-thirds of the class was locating reference materials and completing the EDL program, the other third was shown a filmstrip entitled, *The Reader's Guide*, available at St. Louis A-V Department.

Objective: "After viewing the filmstrip on *The Reader's Guide* students should be able to locate articles in magazines as directed by the abbreviations and symbols used in *The Reader's Guide to Periodical Literature*." After presentation of the filmstrip by the librarian, students were directed to apply the ideas illuminated in the filmstrip to a number of practical exercises.

DAY FIVE

The fourth day schedule was followed. The three groups were rotated and worked simultaneously in three different activities.

The following Monday, I instructed the class that they would be given until Wednesday to complete any assignments they had not finished.

On the fourth day following the final lesson of that unit, students took a twenty-five question criterion test pertaining to reference sources, research thinking patterns, and sound library reference procedures. Out of one hundred students, only eleven missed from one to three more questions than the acceptable minimum of eight.

The social studies teacher concluded the main body of his report with this paragraph:

> This initial experiment pointed up a strong need for systematic library skill training. No instructor should expect his students to operate in the library with any degree of efficiency without prior training and orientation. However, when a librarian and a subject matter instructor plan and work together, state objectives precisely, genuine learning on the part of students can take place and real enthusiasm can be generated.

It is hoped that the brief report of the above joint social science-library project has given you further evidence of the types of "crops" harvested from the "seeding down" of concepts and skills of systematic instructional planning.

TWO

Applying the power of systematic planning

Based on the preceding report of the training sessions held with our staff and samples of planning they produced, you should begin to have an idea of what we mean by systematic planning.

Your next question might well be: How did we prevent this staff in-service from being just a flash in the pan? In other words, how did we solve the puzzle of "transitory responsiveness", which we noted earlier as a dilemma faced by all curriculum planners?

Our direct, gross answer at this time is: Those in-service events and the concomitant new conditions which emerged in our district *accelerated* the use of instructional planning behaviors already present in many of our staff in some incipient form. And it was the *further change of working style of staff that persisted and grew* as staff found it more rewarding to themselves personally and found it more successful in fostering the student performances they wanted to see.

The purpose of this chapter will be to clarify further just what this changed working style was and to highlight some of the changed conditions which encouraged its spread throughout our district. An additional purpose will be to begin to imply our assessment of the values gained by students, teachers, parents, principals, central office personnel, and outside lay and professional persons through the use of systematic instructional planning. Obviously, this latter evaluation will not be closed by this book. It remains an open question in our district even as you read this.

Influencing a change in working style

Knowingly or not, we had adopted a particular mix of existing psychological and sociological theory as we organized the materials and methods for our in-service program on systematic instructional planning. In doing so, we had settled on *our* answer to another of the dilemmas mentioned earlier, namely, the present lack of any clear-cut scientific knowledge about how to change human behavior.

Our adopted theory and its accompanying strategies, in retrospect, were very close to those espoused by B. F. Skinner in his recent book, *Beyond Dignity and Freedom*. It may be said that in general we took on the approach of changing staff behavior by changing the environment in which they worked. Our particular target of changed behavior was to make staff and others more inventive in curriculum making.

Our theoretical position was this: If you want to change staff behavior, you make changes in the school district environment which will (1) model the behavior you want, (2) stimulate and support the effort to use it, and (3) reward its use with consequences that increase the freedom, power, and pleasure of the user.

Now let us continue our examination of how this approach to curriculum improvement was used and its impact on persons, things, and activities in our district.

Applying the "golden triangle" of instructional planning: behavioral objectives, criterion tests, and enabling activities

One way to assemble evidence regarding a school system's application of the idea of systematic instructional planning is to collect data on changes occurring in its criteria and procedures for evaluating student progress. This is by no means a new thought. Educational philosophers and curriculum specialists for many years have been telling us that our basis and methods for grading students are the most significant determiners of the character of our educational program and learning environment.

Not too long ago, a superior intermediate teacher of one of our nongraded, continuous-progress schools distributed a report of the revised evaluation and reporting system being tried that year in grades five and six. The final form of the evaluation instruments had been developed by that teacher during the summer as a part of her course work with Dr. Arthur Wirth at Washington University.

Included here are a few of the introductory remarks of that report and a brief description of the criteria used in her evaluation instruments. It is my feeling that all of this data speaks directly to our question of how the concepts, skills, and attitudes of systematic instructional planning, when applied, will affect the total system of education; i.e., the total learning environment of the learner.

EVALUATION AND REPORTING

In learning to better meet the needs of each child in the classroom, it becomes necessary for the teacher to find better ways to sharpen her perception of what each child is doing. In order to do this, instruments need to be developed to help a teacher observe behavior and changes of behavior of individual children. This evaluation is made primarily to help the teacher constantly revise and restructure the learning situation. [It] will endeavor to report what a student knows and can do, stated behaviorally. . . . This instrument would be used for teacher-parent conferences, as background information for individual cumulative records, and as the framework for written reports to parents.

We will hope that as a result of this year's work, we will, as teachers, have learned to "see" more, and then learn to do something about what we see. Hopefully, we will develop an instrument for self-learning on the part of teachers as well as a device for evaluating children. By sharing this day-to-day progress with children, we hope *they* will learn about self-evaluation, and modify behavior as a result of the evaluation.

The "Instrument for Evaluation" itself contained twenty-five desired types of student behaviors grouped à la Bloom and Gagnè under the headings of "Cognitive Outcomes" and "Personal and Social Development."

Criteria for the evaluation of teachers have also been affected in our district. Our Teacher Evaluation and Salary Program has operated in Ladue since 1953. Associated with the development and implementation of this program has been a statement of criteria and procedures whereby administrators evaluate teachers and assign salary increments rewarding them "on the basis of competency, experience, training, and over-all value to the school system." This "statement" is twenty pages long plus forms and special historical reports.

One year after our work on behavioral objectives, a sixth grade teacher and an elementary principal developed a 15-page *Resource Supplement* to the *Evaluation Criteria and Procedures Booklet*. The purpose of this supplement was to re-define evidences of superior teaching in observable terms and thus offer both teacher and administrator more precision in their cooperative task of evaluating and cultivating teacher competence.

The supplement was divided into four parts:

Part I.   Planning Instruction
Part II.   Establishing Learning Activities
Part III.   Providing Instructional Resources, and
Part IV.   Evaluating Teaching Effectiveness Through Student Behavior

In the excerpts from this document which follow, it should be noted that Part I was based very much on Mager's *Preparing Instructional Objectives*.

The Committee on Evaluation Criteria and Procedures

Part I. Planning Instruction
Truly effective teaching is an outgrowth of careful, conscious planning. The teacher, in planning, must articulate the content, the strategies, and the needs of the student. Hence, planning produces a set of internal directions subject to the constant re-definition demanded by the multiple interactions of the teaching-learning situation.

The effective teacher:
  A. Locates and interprets information on how to write behavioral objectives.

    B. Expresses objectives in terms of expected student performance.
    C. Analyzes each stated objective with such questions as:
        1. Does the objective describe the educational intent clearly?
        2. Does the objective define the criterion of acceptable performance?
    D. Plans thoroughly enough so that each student knows what is expected of him. . . . etc., E through L.

Parts II and III of this document are based very much on Gagnè's *The Conditions of Learning*. Part IV draws heavily from Bloom's *Taxonomy of Cognitive Skills*. The "introduction" to Part IV is excerpted herewith:

> *Part IV. Evaluating Teaching Effectiveness Through Student Behavior*
>
> An important aid to the teacher in assessing his total effectiveness in the teaching-learning process is to focus upon the observable behavior of the students. The student reacts to his environment in such a way as to reflect the organization and planning of instruction activities by the teacher. The purpose of this section is to summarize many of the favorable student performances in behavioral terms so a teacher might recognize his own successes and/or further opportunities for improvement.

Only one closing comment seems warranted at this point. The application of these criteria of superior teaching by teachers in self-evaluation and/or by administrators in our teacher evaluation *system* will assure that the concepts of Mager, Gagnè, and Bloom exert a continuing influence on the character of the learning environments in our schools.

The guideline to be inferred from the preceding illustrations is that *curriculum planning must have sufficient impact to influence the evaluation system of the school system if it is to be effective and if it is to endure*. In fact, the basic rationale (new purposes) of any revised curriculum must effect correlative changes in all systems, administrative, personnel, financial, and special services, as well as instructional, if significantly improved learning environments are to be implemented and maintained.

Later applications of systematic planning in major curriculum revision projects

A different and interesting kind of evidence of the "utilization" of systematic planning can be found in the revised K-12 Visual Arts Program completed in 1969 by our art staff under the dynamic leadership of the Coordinator of Art Education. The art coordinator had this to say in the preface of the new teacher's guide:

> The Ladue art staff has designed a behaviorally oriented, quality program of art education with concern for the affective domain as well as the cognitive domain of learning.

Mager's recent book, *Developing Attitudes Toward Learning*, was a very practical help to the staff in identifying and describing behaviors which would indicate positive attitudes toward art experiences in school and toward an aesthetic perspective of life in general.

The two parts of the voluminous art guide to be cited here are (1) the staff's assumptions about the value of behavioral objectives and (2) a sample planning sheet which demonstrates how behavioral objectives were used to organize and to communicate classroom experiences in the area of art.

Many guidelines for effective curriculum planning are forcefully implied in what the art staff had to say about behavioral objectives as a basis for instruction:

> Why behavioral objectives? Behavioral objectives have very great appeal for these reasons:
> 1. Some form of effective and useful life-behavior is the real goal of education. Most of our present "knowledge" objectives are nothing more than intermediate steps toward those goals and often have no demonstrable power to contribute to the goals. In contrast, if we achieve a behavioral objective, we have really affected out-of-school behavior in a very direct way. The transfer potential of a behavioral objective is very high. . . . etc., 2 through 3.
> 4. *Clearly stated behaviors* which meet the criterion herein

presented remove all the guesswork for the teacher from the identification of relevant content . . . Thus we can select from the overwhelming mass of factual information that which is of most value for human behavior and assign *priorities on the basis of usefulness*. . . . etc. through 5.

6. When a behavioral objective has been fully stated and its component *concepts* and *subcompetencies* have been identified, it proves to be an excellent pre-instructional diagnostic test as well as the final measure of achievement.

In summary, behavioral objectives are so closely aligned with the basic principles of human behavior and learning, and so intimately related to the practical needs of people, that they offer a way of making instruction easier to plan, easier to carry out, and more effective in influencing human life.

I have chosen a second grade lesson (see Figure 2-1) to show (1) the pivotal role of behavioral objectives in the development of art experiences and (2) the format of the planning sheet used to communicate these ideas to all staff, present and future.

Figure 2-1. Art Planning Sheet

Area of Study_____ Painting _____

Carrier Project_____ Mixed Media Mural _____

Suggested Grade Level_____ 2 _____

BEHAVIORAL OBJECTIVES

(Intended Outcomes for the Student)

The learner will be able to:

1. Explain one function of a mural with respect to where it will be displayed.
2. Explain the organization of a city (city planning).
3. Increase his awareness of the following surroundings:
   a) architecture (different structures serve different purposes)
   b) landscape (in relation to the buildings)
   c) placement and development of streets, sidewalks, and water-ways to accommodate modes of transportation.
   d) natural and man-made elements existing together (one work-

ing advantageously for the other).
4. Work with others (sharing ideas) as a significant part of a group, just as we are all members of a community.
5. Integrate a variety of media into one complete expression (mixed media experience).
6. (If he is a painter) mix primary colors (and black and white) in order to create new colors and discover that there are many variations of each color.
7. Discriminate between the sizes of structures in relation to each other.

Materials Needed

Student:	Teacher:
1. 15 feet of brown mural paper	Conference with classroom teacher to find out material covered in social studies unit of "The Community."
2. White chalk	
3. Tempera paint: red, yellow, blue, black, white	
4. Asst. colors of construction paper	
5. Pencils, crayons, scissors, glue, magic markers, large paint brushes	
6. Jars of water (for painting)	

TEACHING STRATEGIES
(Motivation and Procedure)

1. *Motivation*: Open discussion defining the make-up of a community. Let students determine (with guidance) the basic different areas of town. Divide students into committees representing these areas: residential, business district, educational and recreational, and landscape (for the first 3 areas). Each committee elects a chairman.
2. *Activity*:
   a) Landscape committee paints land on mural that will accomodate the community. Sketch layout first with chalk. Having them mix their own colors will help them discover there are many variations of each color, and leaves the teacher open to ask (e.g.) "Is grass always one color only?"
   b) Other committees decide specifically on types of buildings to be made for their area. Use construction paper to

create shape of structure, and pencils, crayons, and magic markers to put in detail.

c) Committee chairmen work together on establishing sizes of structures and landscape that are relative to one another.

d) Entire class decides in a discussion on assembling buildings on landscape. Several students glue structures onto mural paper at a time.

EVALUATION TECHNIQUE
(Acceptable Performance)

1. Observation of student:
   a) in working as an active participant of the group.
   b) in his degree of awareness of the type of structure he is creating.
   c) in his ability to relate the size of his structure to the others.
   d) as to whether or not he attempted (as a painter) mixing primary colors to get the colors he needed.
2. Observation of complete group mural to see if "The Community" is well organized and functional.

Nota Bene:
1. Shoes off when painting on mural paper!

Supporting systematic planning with flow charts and planning sheets

Between the years of 1964 and 1966, an increased need arose to find practical ways to give special guidance and support to systematic instructional planning. As one consequence, in the spring of 1966 we applied for a P.L. 89-10 Title III planning grant "to plan a supplementary educational center and services." What we proposed was the development of the Ladue Instructional Planning Center. We did *not* receive the grant, but we *did* develop and are still operating the IPC as proposed.

As stated in the grant proposal, the purpose of the center was to provide optimum conditions for doing continuous instructional planning including three essential ingredients: (1) specific guidance in the procedures of systematic, instructional planning within the context of a stated philosophy and agreed-upon, over-all curricular structure, (2) readily accessible, substantive resources and production services, and (3) unencumbered time. The basic rationale of the proposal said that professional and lay leadership, to be effective in changing the learning experiences in the classroom, *must intervene at the point of instructional planning being done by the teacher*.

At this point, it seems most appropriate to share with you the flow chart and planning sheets which the IPC staff currently uses to assist summer teams in their production of instructional materials.

The flow chart (see Figures 2-2, 2-3, 2-4, and 2-5) extends from step 1, initial orientation sessions, to step 16, completion of the project happily signaled by the presentation of supplementary salary checks to weary team members. Our actual flow chart is an 11"x 17" two-side print with the chart on one side and the description of each step on the back. For the purposes of this report, I have chosen to print the flow chart and descriptions together. As indicated in the key, a circle represents the writing team, a triangle represents the special subject coordinator who is the central office liaison person between the team and the IPC, and the square represents the IPC personnel and services including research, libraries, graphics, AV production, typing services, and print shop.

Figure 2-2. Flow Chart for Instructional Planning and Production

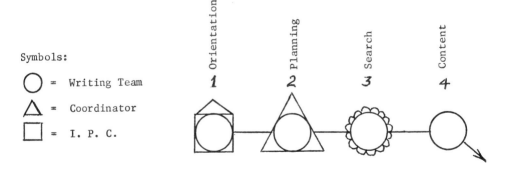

1. *Orientation*. Define task of team. Identify roles of team members, coordinators, and IPC. Make an initial listing of available resources. Plan time and space for working. Examine scope and constraints of project. Project next steps.

2. *Planning*. Refine original planning to more specific expected outcomes. Project general visualization of final product. Plan considerations for nature of the learner, rationale, basic aims, objectives, a variety of teaching strategies and materials, and format.

3. *Search*. Make a substantial search for available commercial materials. Research content area and related concepts through IPC, Libraries, Surveys (teachers and students), Catalogs, County AV, and other college and community resources. Reduce material to a few alternatives.

4. *Content*. Select the general content area to be included in project. Define the concepts to be developed. Develop main topics and related sub-topics.

Figure 2-3. Flow Chart for Instructional Planning and Production (*Continued*)

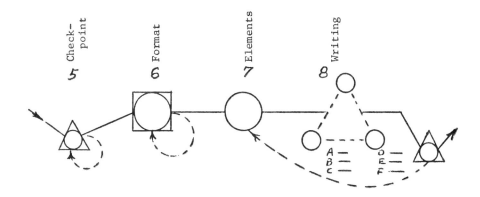

5. *Checkpoint A*. Coordinators are to assist in future planning by asking: Is content related to level of learner, related to rationale, relevant to other units in the same area of curriculum, reasonable within time allotted for teaching and learning, and are concepts well documented?

6. *Format*. In what form will material be presented to learner, and what will Teacher's Resource include? Then communicate with the IPC to discuss and plan physical characteristics and appearance of unit. The IPC director is to establish procedure with typists and artists to work from rough to finished copy.

7. *Elements*. Divide larger content area into several smaller pieces. Select and sequence specific content elements to be developed. Proper selection of content elements leads to better learning development and motivation.

8. *Writing*. Start the writing phase, relating each lesson to the specific content. Include the behavioral objectives, teaching strategies, and materials and techniques of evaluating the outcomes of the lesson. This step is to be *repeated* as many times as necessary to complete the project.

Figure 2-4. Flow Chart for Instructional Planning and Production (Continued)

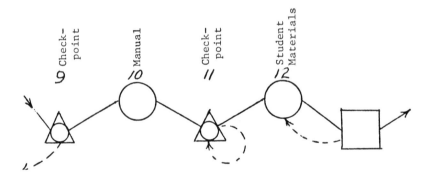

9. *Checkpoint B*. Coordinators are to assist in evaluating each lesson as to clarity of objectives, and the sequence of lessons related to learning theory. Added teaching strategies and materials may be suggested to provide a variety of motivating learning experiences.

10. *Manual*. Complete Teacher's Manual with all necessary teacher resource information. Teacher prep-sheets and introductory notes are effective to convey proper teaching attitude. All material must be numbered, and a table of contents is useful.

11. *Checkpoint C*. Coordinators are to provide an evaluation of Teacher's Manual, checking format and whether or not the writer's intent was properly described in the manual.

12. *Student Materials*. Complete all student materials which are to be duplicated or printed. Also complete all other teaching materials such as: transparencies, tapes, slides, pictures, worksheets, laminated cards, etc.

Figure 2-5. Flow Chart for Instructional Planning and Production (Continued)

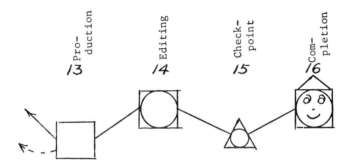

13. *Production*. Check with the IPC for final production plans. Supply all necessary instructions as to printing: paper size, color of paper, color of ink, type of binding, number of copies, etc.

14. *Editing*. Proof read all finished mats and material. Most problems in producing a finished product are created by improper editing procedures. Care must be taken in handling finished mats to enhance best appearance in finished products.

15. *Checkpoint D*. The coordinators are to check completed

project. Writers are to list all items which have not yet been completed, and expected completion dates.

16. *Completion.* Plans are formulated for distribution of completed materials. This step marks the climax of the "writing-production" phase and the commencement of the "piloting-implementing" stage.

The processing and approval of IPC summer projects usually occurs sometime between March and May of each school year. Approved projects have been from one to six weeks for a particular production, each involving from one to as many as eight authors. We have learned that two-member teams are most productive. Consequently, when the job is a large one, we involve many people by breaking the work assignments into many parts which can be done simultaneously by several two-member working teams.

Later descriptions of specific projects will reveal the many levels and forms of assistance that are necessary as a school district ventures further and further into the business of producing its own curriculum and instructional materials.

Considering the untapped resource, the student

Nowhere in the 1966 grant proposal for the IPC was mention made of the involvement of students in the early decisions of curriculum development and instructional planning. In recent years, in our district we have begun formally to recognize that one of the missing ingredients in instructional planning is input from the learners themselves. This is an embarrassing admission on the part of a curriculum coordinator with a professed philosophy of wanting to devise instruction more responsive to the needs and expressed interests of the learner. Traditionally, students have been involved only at the point of teacher-pupil planning in the classroom.

During a recent spring cycle, I surveyed teams submitting IPC proposals regarding the involvement of students in curriculum planning. The responses to my inquiry ranged from merely questions about what I meant to extensive descriptions of ways in which students had been involved. Let me summarize some of their responses as a way of suggesting to you some guidelines for the involvement of students in curriculum planning.

As might be expected, some traditional ways for involving students were among those suggested. A journalism teacher reported that present students would be asked what specific areas they felt would be of interest to future journalism students. This teacher also thought it would be a good idea to have two or three students check the first drafts of new instructional packages in order to point out sections unclear to them.

The teacher of our high school course in psychology had students rate the interest and degree of growth which they experienced in the case of each unit of the course. She asked them for suggestions to improve their interest and growth.

The teacher applying for time to revise two drama courses sent the following note:

Dr. Morley—

Although I have not turned anything in to the IPC as yet, I have the main body of my planning done. I have talked quite a bit with my directing class this year about curriculum. After their One-Acts are over, I will go over my plans with them to see if they see any problems. I have also talked with my Acting III class and will do so again before I do any further planning on that course. In talking with these classes, I have asked for their ideas and sounded out mine.

If you feel that I have not involved them enough in planning, please let me know.

Janet

The chairman of the team of four working on the development of a new course in cinema reported that the team intended to use material prepared by a recent graduate who had been conducting film festivals at his university. Also, this teacher reported that an upperclass English student had been encouraged to use his independent study time in writing several tentative packages for the new course.

The most extensive response came from the chairman of a three-member team who had applied for several weeks to redevelop the entire tenth grade World History course, which uses closed-circuit TV for its lecture sessions. This chairman sent me copies of the survey instruments they were using with students and the analyses of what they found in those cases where the survey had been completed. One set of instruments pertained to student evaluation of the different textbooks being used in regular and pilot classes. The other activity reported was a statistical study of student intellectual growth through the use of a locally designed criterion test of fifteen multiple-choice items testing intellectual skills.

Even though it would not be too difficult to be critical of the research design and statistical analysis made by this team, what they did can be credited as an honest attempt to use measurements of student response as a guide for curriculum planning.

Let me add one most recent illustration of student involvement in curriculum planning. Fourteen high school students enrolled in the quarter course, "Grammar," chose as a class project the rewriting of the sophomore semester course, "Composition I," which all of them had taken as sophomores. After reviewing, discussing, and projecting possible changes on the basis of their own experience, the teacher arranged for two of the students to confer with seven ninth grade students who would be taking the course the next year. This conference was conducted by the visiting upperclassmen, who came prepared with several questions for checking out how correctly they had anticipated the attitudes, interests, needs, and competencies of entering students. In addition, they asked for the ninth graders' critique of the allocation of time given to different types of composition and their ideas of topics upon which they would most like to read and write essays.

This seemed to be an exemplary case of "feed forward" in curriculum planning. Some curriculum projects call this "learner verification and revision."

Despite the illustrations above, it would appear that we have a long way to go in devising effective means for involving students in this phase of our work. Individual teachers must be credited with much informal and indirect involvement, which has contributed visibly to what effectiveness and relevance exists in our present instructional programs.

Evaluating the kind and quality of systematic planning in the summer of 1970 as a criterion check of over-all progress

How was the IPC faring after five years? What kinds of projects were being pursued and how did they measure up in terms of the purposes expressed in the 1966 grant application?

First, let me insert a note about our revised reward system as a follow-up to my opening remarks (Chapter I) about how a change in a reward system is one kind of environmental change which can bring about changes in human behavior. Organization of the center brought two new financial rewards into the picture, plus the prestige reward of being selected as a district author of curriculum materials.

The two financial rewards were supplementary summer salaries and the possibility of pro-rated financial returns from sales to other districts. Later on, more will be said about these arrangements.

Now let me provide some vital statistics on IPC production during the summer of 1970.

Summer 1970 New IPC Applications

Submitted by Teacher Teams	-	*19*
Approved	-	7
Amended and Approved	-	10
Not approved	-	2
Other Summer 1970 Projects Completed	-	*24*
Central office curriculum guide	-	2
Non-sponsored pilot materials	-	1
Administrative handbooks	-	5
Reruns of earlier publications	-	16

Forty-one teachers received supplementary salaries totaling about $15,000 for their work on approved *sponsored* IPC projects. The sponsored projects spread over the curriculum as follows:

Special education	-	1
Practical arts	-	1
Fine arts	-	4
Language arts	-	5
Social studies	-	6
Total	-	17

This clearly revealed the current emphasis on the humanities in contrast to the push in mathematics and science in the early 60's.

The two publications developed by the central office were a *Teacher's Handbook for Social Studies K-12 and a Guide to AV Materials Available from the IPC for Use in Sex Education K-6*. In both cases we had arrived at a point of wrapping up a development extending over five years. The publications would help to consolidate and maintain gains realized to that point.

I am reminded of the dilemma of individual and group morale mentioned earlier. These above publications represent one form of communication used by many school districts to strengthen a staff's commitment to a carefully developed and agreed-upon program.

The unsponsored summer project was a comprehensive spelling text to be piloted by volunteer elementary and secondary evaluators. The IPC furnished the production services and supplies for this workbook but did not pay the author a supplementary salary. Under this arrangement the District allows the author full ownership rights to the materials should he want to sell it to a commercial publisher. For its part of the bargain, the District retains written permission from the author to reproduce and use the experimental edition as long as a commercial version is not available.

In the case of sponsored projects where authors are paid a supplementary salary, the authors and districts sign a copyright agreement as follows:

_____ Approved by Executive Committee, LIPC
    Date

All materials produced by you (or your team) from work on the project listed above shall be the property of the school district and shall not be used, published or sold without the written consent of the school district.

If you are working as a single applicant, the school district will pay you one-half of all royalties or other payments received from the publication and sale of any project materials during your lifetime for any such income grossing $100 or more.

In the case of a team project, one-half of all royalties or other payments, grossing $100 or more, received from the publication and sale of any project materials shall be paid in equal shares to the members of the team. Upon the death of a team member, his or her share shall be retained by the school district.

Unless the school district consents otherwise, all publications of any materials (including books) shall bear the following legend on the title page, the reverse side thereof, or an appropriate, visible placement in the case of A-V materials:

"School District of the City of Ladue 1967"

—(or other year of publication)

School Superintendent	Applicant's Signature	Date

The five administrative handbooks were either staff handbooks for a given secondary school or special district-wide handbooks to be used as a part of our district's teacher evaluation program. The IPC's involvement was to secure supplies for the printing and binding, to assist in the layout of covers and some special pages, and to schedule the print shop run to assure production and distribution as per the preset target date.

Reruns of all or parts of earlier curriculum publications had become a sizable recurring production item by our fifth summer of operation. It should be noted that by that time it had become standard procedure to anticipate such reruns as early as possible, and to have many printed during slack times between January and June.

The sixteen reruns scheduled during the summer of 1970 happened to be the following:

Student booklets and/or worksheets for *eleven* elementary social studies units.

An experimental edition of a consummable individualized spelling workbook.

Student worksheets for year-long, locally developed courses in *7th* and *8th* grade science.

Student worksheets for IPC Black Literature course.
Student instructional packages for complete course in Russian History.

On the concluding pages of this chapter I have reprinted brief, selected sections of five of the 1970 products so that you can make your own assessment of our success in guiding teams toward the use of systematic instructional planning.

The first is from the category of *special education*. A first grade teacher and our special service director prepared 75 lesson plans, 20 transparencies with accompanying worksheets, and descriptions of 44 "crafty ideas" lessons to be used for visual-motor training in grade two, the school year 1970-71. Those materials were developed as part of the instructional input in our 4-year district research study of the relationship of different instructional modes to different learning styles. An instructional objective and the teaching strategies of a sample lesson follow.

BEHAVIORAL OBJECTIVES
FOR VISUAL-MOTOR TRAINING

B. *Visual Coordination and Pursuit:* The ability to follow and track objects and symbols with coordinated eye movements.

With head steady, pupil can move eyes to fixate on stable objects in varied places, pursue moving objects such as finger positions, follow picture and word stories left to right without jerky movements.

TEACHING STRATEGIES

The teacher will:
1. ask the children to use the pictures on p. 8 (a commercial text) to complete the sentences on p. 9.
2. write complete sentences on the chalkboard.
3. encourage good posture and head position by playing a game. Instruct the children to: sit up at your desk with your head held steady and your right hand flat on the desk. Now look at what I tell you: "thumb-chalkboard, first-finger chalkboard, middle finger-chalkboard, ring finger-chalkboard, little finger-

chalkboard.'' Repeat this with left hand in order from little finger to thumb. Each time you call out chalkboard, point to one of the words in the sentences you have written.

4. explain to the children that good posture will enable them to copy the words they need easier and more quickly.
5. encourage them to practice moving their eyes rather than their heads as they copy the sentences.
6. pass out tracing paper as they finish and tell them to begin to trace the picture on p. 8.
7. direct those who finish early to color the pictures they have made.

N.B. The object here is to develop fine muscle control by tracing and to develop the ability to copy from the board by moving the eyes up and down, minimizing head movement.

The second sample of instructional planning is from the category of practical arts. Under a 3-week summer project our chairman of business education completed the overall plans for a new course, Business Information and Data Processing. I have selected excerpts from "student goals" and "student activities," all from the first part of Unit II of this new course. In this case the teacher was planning for himself and his students alone, since he was the only one teaching this course during the 1970-71 school year. Once he had fieldtested his new course and needed to write plans that other teachers could use, he would be asked to produce a more complete, interrelated set of specific behavioral objectives, teaching strategies, and evaluation techniques. With that said, I will let you be the judge of what he did produce, at least in terms of the limited sample displayed below.

STUDENT GOALS
UNIT II

Students will explain unit record processing, its purpose and mechanics.

Students will distinguish between unit record and computer data processing.

Students will explain the varying data-processing needs dependent upon size, volume, and type of operation performed.

STUDENT ACTIVITIES

UNIT II

Answer the following questions:

What is a unit record?

What are the measurements of a punch card?

Define the terms *edge* and *face*, . . . etc.

Organize the following key-punch components into proper order based on the path of the card:

punch station

card stacker

read station

List some of the reasons for verification.

Define and explain the interpreting function . . . etc.

Indicate the path of a card through an interpreter.

Explain why classification plays an important part in unit-record processing.

Point out examples of classification in your school.

Explain the purpose of a reproducer.

List the documents you may have to have reproduced during your lifetime . . . etc.

Next we go to the category of fine arts. I shall let the teacher's introduction speak for itself, then follow with some of the table of contents and a bit of one lesson. All of these are from the student's book.

The available music theory textbooks were too complex and advanced to be comprehensible to the high school student. The available recordings and scores by themselves would have tended to confuse rather than to educate. Therefore, the instructor created a 77-page student book for *Music Theory I* and a 55-page booklet for *Music Theory II*, which he felt would give high school students a sound introduction to the concepts, structure, symbols, vocabulary, and repertory of traditional harmony.

I believe that the following excerpts give a representative sampling of these instructional materials.

INTRODUCTION

Music Theory I is a course of study concerned with the harmonic materials and formal structure of the music of the 17th, 18th, and 19th centuries, i.e. the "traditional harmony" of the western European cultures. . . .

The student is cautioned against interpreting this instruction as a finite course in music theory. At best this can be considered only an introduction to harmony and form. Of necessity, a great deal of ground is being covered in a relatively short period of time because most students will not be able to include more than one year of theory in their three years of high school. . . .

CONTENTS

UNIT I - PREPARATORY MATERIAL

UNIT I

Harmonic Progression by Descending 5th: The cadence **V-I** (Authentic) suggests the possibility of arranging all the triads of the diatonic scale in a descending 5th relationship, culminating with I. The harmonic progression thus obtained is the strongest and most important of progressions.

IV   VII   III   VI   II   V   I

In this music example the ascending 4th, which is the inversion of the descending 5th, is substituted alternately for the 5th to keep the progression within the range of the bass clef.

Play the progression several times. Notice the symmetry established by the root sequence of 5ths, and the apparent inevitability and drive to the tonic . . . etc.

Our fourth example is from the category of language arts. Reproduced next are a few beginning parts of Package III, Semantics. This is one page of a 6-page unipac out of the four unipacs which make up a new *quarter course* in linguistics, titled Dynamics of Language. Under the "innovation" schedule in our high school students attend, in a two-week period, *one* large group lecture, *five* small group seminars, and *four* independent study periods which include at least one conference with the teacher every three weeks. The unipac is the major guide for the student during his work on this four-week unit.

GHOTI Spells Fish

Package III: Semantics
Suggested Time: 3-4 weeks (10 seminar sessions)
    I. *Purpose:*
        The purpose of this package is to study the uses of language as a tool and to distinguish the different ways in which people consciously employ it to achieve their specific intent.

II. *Goals:*
   A. To recognize the symbolic nature of language.
   B. To review the difference between denotation and con-
   notation.
   C. To review the way one's experience shapes his lan-
   guage . . .etc.
   J. To accept that everyone brings his own understanding,
   background, and "bias" to his experiences and his
   statements about those experiences.
   K. To have fun with words.
III. *Student Activities and Procedures:*
   A. Attend large group sessions and take relevant notes.
   The large group presentations often clarify topics discussed in seminars and provide ideas for projects.
   B. Keep a notebook (study notes, project materials,
   seminar work) which you will bring to seminars and
   to conferences with your teacher. *Caution:* Since you
   may be asked to turn in your notebook at the end of
   the quarter, do not discard any sections which are
   relevant to the course.
   C. Confer with your seminar teacher once during the
   time you are working on this package.
   D. Read Chapters 6; 9-12; 14; in *Looking at Language*
   and be prepared to express your understanding of and
   responses to the topics under discussion. *Note: Be
   certain to check ahead in the discussion questions
   and exercises to know whether you are expected to
   have read certain chapters or to bring items.*

The final sample is drawn from the category of social studies.
The summer of 1970 signaled the near-completion of a total revision
of our K-12 social studies. The materials displayed here come from
the revised twelve-week unit on geography taught in all seventh
grade classes. The unit is composed of four weeks in each of three
aspects of geography: physical, population, and economic. I have
chosen to exhibit some parts of Lesson A of Unit I—Physical
Geography. Shown are some of the instructions in the teacher's
manual. I regret that there was no easy way to reprint a portion
of the two-color topographical map produced by the IPC as a student
worksheet in this lesson.

UNIT I–PHYSICAL GEOGRAPHY

LESSON A

2 days

Objectives:

1. Using appropriate given symbols, students will record on school site maps the location of physical features, both natural and man-made, and public services, such as water hydrants, sewers, and public telephones.
2. Using a compass, students will record the north, south, east, and west directions of their map.
3. Using a yardstick, students will measure a wall of the school building, calculate and record the scale of their maps.
4. Using their completed maps, students will describe orally the following aspects of their school setting: natural resources (including plant and animal life), estimated residential populations, types of man-made facilities, economic operations, and public services.
5. Reviewing the information recorded on their maps, the students will list the tasks and problems faced by the cartographer.
6. Keep a vocabulary notebook.

Procedures:

1. Hand out maps (Handout #1) to students.
2. Explain briefly the use of the symbols which appear in the key or legend of the map . . . etc.
3. Divide the class into five smaller groups with the assignment of reporting orally to the whole class on one of the five subassignments of Objective 4. (See above.)
4. Be certain the students understand that all of them should show direction and scale on their maps, as well as location of principal physical features. . . .
5. Make prior decision about most useful route to be followed on walking field trip. . . .
6. For reporting purposes, a chairman from each small group could be the spokesman, with the others contributing and answering questions.

Evaluation:

The teacher may regard the recordings on individual maps and the oral reports of each group as a means of ascertaining the success of each student in the lesson.

If the excerpts from the IPC projects of the summer of 1970 have served my intended purpose, they have enabled you to determine your own answer to the question: Did the IPC provide the three essential ingredients for optimum instructional planning, namely, guidance on systematic planning, supporting research and production services, and unencumbered time.

THREE

Developing and coordinating curriculum planning teams

In this chapter we will examine the coordination and nurture of curriculum planning teams. We will look at four functional aspects of this process and will suggest how a facilitator can deal adequately with each of these.

I would hazard the guess that most of us have already realized the complexity of coordinating multiple planning groups. It makes little difference whether such coordination is done by a director for a district, a principal for a school, a teacher for a group of youngsters, or a parent for a household. The experience of the leader-facilitator will be quite similar in each case.

We will be trying to answer the basic question: How does one assert some measure of quality control over such a complex process?

Attending to four functional aspects of coordination

Curriculum coordination is (1) goal-directed, (2) cyclic, (3) cooperative, and (4) productive of people-growth and program-development. A professional cultivation of the process requires proper attention to each of these four functional aspects of coordination. Evidence of effective attention should be visible in the several formal and semi-formal arrangements established in a given situation to facilitate each of these functions.

The goal-directed aspect of curriculum coordination is attended to by seeing that purposes (objectives) of programs are agreed upon *before* efforts are focused in any intense fashion on the selection and/or creation of the form of the new program. The guideline, therefore, is to give careful attention to the procedures and supporting conditions that allow a planning group to arrive at a most valid and near-unanimous agreement regarding the objectives to be attained by a revised program.

The cyclical aspect of curriculum coordination merely acknowledges the phases of goal setting, of curriculum planning, of instructional implementation, and of outcome evaluation that operate over cycles of time. Each of these phases is relatively different and requires different kinds of guidance and support. The guideline, therefore, is to have techniques which keep you informed of the current phase of each curriculum project and which assist you in providing the appropriate support services for the current phases of each project, even though they are at different points in the developmental cycle. A simplified diagram for a cycle of continuous curriculum renewal is shown in Figure 3-1.

This matter of time cycles can indeed be challenging. Let me cite just one kind of problem which coordinators, principals, and teachers face regularly. I am thinking of the fact that we must continually revitalize traditionally "established" curriculums, such as a survey American history course, as well as invent contemporary "emerging" curriculums such as American issues, an integration of the study of American history with experiences in clarifying the value conflicts in past and present public issues. Both types of coordination must be supported simultaneously. The "emerging" curriculum sometimes captivates our interest to such an extent that we allow *premature* deterioration in the existing courses; that is, prior to their displacement by a well-designed, well-proven revised curriculum.

The particular guideline here is that the instructional leader must acquire the tact and techniques to keep a viable "established"

Figure 3-1. Curriculum Renewal Cycle

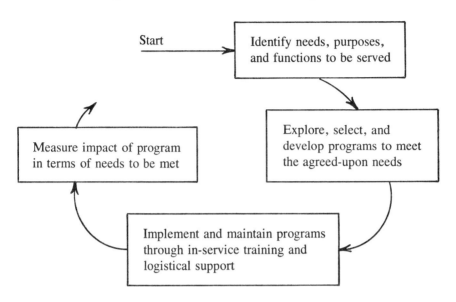

program going during the transition to an "emerging" one. It would appear advisable that the effective coordinator, in his on-going work with colleagues, students, and parents, (1) should keep alerting them to possible future trends (2) while he is aiding them in the development of revised programs (3) as he expands throughout the system the beneficial effect of established programs. Working on revised programs should take only one-third of his time, talent, and energy. Some suggestions of how to do this will be found in Chapter Five, as well as in remaining parts of this one.

A third functional aspect of coordination is that it is a cooperative endeavor. The guideline, therefore, is that on-going cooperation requires organization. For example, the district-wide coordination of *established* curriculums is done through the leadership and cooperative efforts of the *line* members of the instructional staff: superintendent, principals, departmental chairmen, .and teachers. On the other hand, the coordination of *emerging* curriculums may be the primary concern of *staff* persons of the instructional division: instructional coordinators, subject specialists, and selected teachers.

Further, you and I know that sophisticated cooperative efforts frequently require many forms of specialization. Practical considerations often make it necessary to have one group to handle the goal-setting phase of a curriculum project, another group to develop the program, all teachers to implement it, and a separate panel responsible for the evaluation of the program's impact on students. However, a guideline to be specially noted here is that the flow of motivation and insight from one group to another will *not* occur unless there is periodic pre-involvement of "receiving" groups in the on-going deliberations of the "preceding" groups. The lesson here seems to be that any initiating group must take as one of its tasks the early, preliminary involvement of the next group, if the performance of the second is to be a true flowering of the first.

A fourth functional aspect of coordination is that it involves both the growth of people and the development of programs. This means, for example, that in the case of a district-wide, in-service effort, the competent curriculum coordinator must be able to provide environments in which principals and teachers can grow at the same time that improved instructional materials and activities are being produced.

Creating a functional official structure

Basic to all four aspects of coordination is the creation of an organized, regularly scheduled set of functional groups. It is through the active, differentiated roles played by individuals in these groups that a *coordinated* effort is born and sustained.

Since form should follow function, the instructional leader should be most concerned that the structure of each of these groups, the relationships of one to another, and their schedule of meetings, are all formed in such a way as to facilitate all four functional aspects of coordination.

Some wise sociologist has said: "Human actions are not discrete, they occur in systems." Curriculum planning teams are not discrete, and like it or not must plan and operate in systems already existing. Each planned component of change must somehow be reconciled with aspects of existing related systems—such as a physical aspect of a change dove-tailed with the immediate physical systems or a social role change integrated with existing systems of social roles.

Obviously, there is always the possibility of changing operating systems to make them more accommodating to the injection of new subsystems. However, if this is expected, those planners interested in the survival of the inserted sub-system must include in their over-all effort some deliberate procedures for bringing about the needed changes in the existing systems. For if these procedures fail, the incompatibility of the existing system will cause it to reject the innovation regardless of how hard the creative change agent may wish it otherwise.

An important implication of what has just been said is that the change agent, be he coordinator, principal, teacher, student, or parent, must not only be an astute creator of innovations compatible with existing systems, but he must also possess some potency for managing or modifying existing systems to make them more accommodating to the slightly out-of-phase innovation. The several systems I am referring to are everything from the mundane distribution of enclosed space to the esoteric set of postulates underlying the district's philosophy. The innovator is frequently in the position of having to find ways to alter the character of the operational environment. Or, in the words of our agricultural metaphor, he must be able to work the ground as well as sow the seed.

The line and staff position of an instructional leader significantly affects his ability to generate appropriate changes and to implant them securely within existing systems. True to his function, the superintendent of our district has always seen to it that the official line and staff structure of our district is well understood by all staff. He has created a structure (Figure 3-2) having muscle, without its being muscle-bound. It has centralized power when and where control is called for, yet it has allowed a broad front of staff initiative in identifying, analyzing, implementing, and evaluating change.

A few features of this organizational arrangement deserve special comment. First, the line authority from the Board

Figure 3-2.   Line and Staff Organization

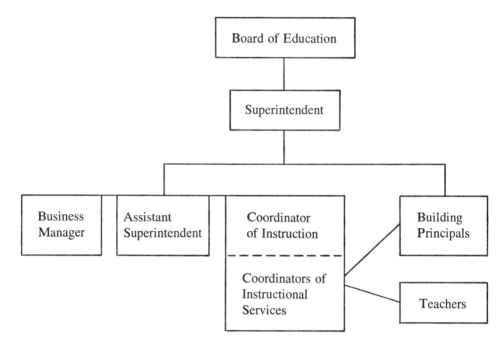

through the superintendent is well established in our situation and is not abused by either party. It is realistic to expect that the current national forces of teacher militancy will ultimately place stress and strain on this arrangement.

Second, the superintendent, as both administrative and educational boss of the district, maintains direct lines of control to his assistant superintendent in the central office and to each of his building principals in the field. Third, each building principal is administrative and educational leader of his staff.

Fourth, and most pertinent to the concerns of this book, the entire instructional division is in a horizontal, staff relationship with building administrators and teachers. Fifth, the triangular subsystem of instructional coordinator, building administrator, and teacher carries the major responsibility for curriculum change and instructional improvement in our district. This triumvirate has representation from each of the three instructional arenas

—the district, the building, and the classroom. When each representative applies his perspective to the planning, the likelihood of a balanced, coordinated program is greatly increased.

Finally, the official structure diagramed here provides the instructional specialist with direct access to all operating systems, but at the same time does not tie up his energies completely with the constant, demanding encumbrances of any particular operating system. Consequently, he can operate in gear and exert influence throughout the status quo, or he can freewheel in some experimental spin, to be engaged with other systems at some later time.

In Figure 3-3 you will see a diagram of what we found to be an effective organization for curriculum coordination at the senior high level. It included a High School Instructional Council composed of the high school principal, his three assistants, the head counselor, all department chairmen, and all instructional coordinators from the central office. Usually, it met every other week, alternating with the principals' meeting with the department chairmen.

Guidelines for coordinating administrative and instructional matters were presented by the high school principal and the coordinator of instruction at the organizational meeting of the High School Instructional Council. As indicated in the diagram, the line of authority for operational decisions flowed two-way from and to the superintendent, principals, department chairmen, and teachers. The coordinating bodies for making decisions about what educational services should be offered and about the conditions under which they should be offered were five in number: the administrative council, the coordinators' council, the high school instructional council, the interschool departmental meetings, and the individual departmental meetings. And finally, it should be noted that there was a line of authority for decisions about in-service programs and curriculum materials flowing two-way from and to coordinators, department chairmen, and teachers.

Two guidelines presented at that meeting are quoted below. They were an attempt to clarify the conditions necessary for instructional coordinators to carry out their unique roles.

V. Subject area and general instructional coordinators have a special responsibility for the development and coordination of instruction across all schools and across all grade levels which requires: (A) full membership on appropriate coordinating bodies, (B) continuous and current information of all major instructional decisions being made in their curricular fields, (C) standing invitation to attend departmental meetings, and (D) active channels through the principals and departmental chairmen for calling interschool departmental meetings, conducting in-service sessions, making class visitations, and arranging conferences with individual or groups of teachers.

VI. Coordinators are on call to the superintendent, principals, and department chairmen for assistance regarding any aspect of instructional services in our schools.

In Figure 3-3, I have attempted to diagram the relationships, roles, and responsibilities of principals, departmental chairmen, teachers, and instructional coordinators.

Similar staff structures and coordinating bodies were created for the other grade levels. However, we did not think it advisable to form groups called the junior high or elementary instructional council. Rather, we had the Junior High Administrative Council and the Elementary Administrative Council each perform dual roles as administrative and instructional coordinating bodies. These councils, when necessary, appointed *ad hoc* steering committees for special tasks which required more constant husbanding than the councils could provide through their once-a-month meetings.

These organizational structures may appear quite typical. Typical or not, let it be reiterated that some such structure is necessary. Slight variations in the arrangement probably make little or no difference. It is the working style of these groups that makes the difference. In the final analysis, leadership is as leadership does, regardless of how it is titled or organized.

Establishing over-all district goals and instituting reasonable authoritative controls over the curriculum renewal process

One spring in the early 60's, the superintendent and board of our district launched a Task Force to generate a clearer forecast of the direction our school system might take in the future. Obvi-

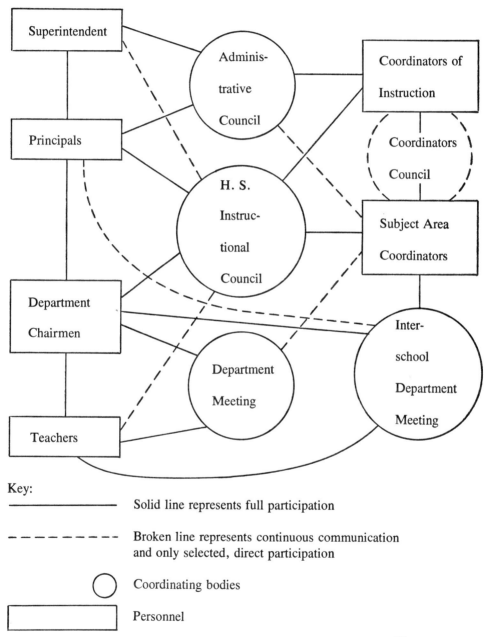

Figure 3-3. Staff Organization and Coordinating Bodies for Instruction, Grades 10-12

Superintendent

Administrative Council

Coordinators of Instruction

Principals

Coordinators Council

H. S. Instructional Council

Subject Area Coordinators

Department Chairmen

Inter-school Department Meeting

Department Meeting

Teachers

Key:

——————————— Solid line represents full participation

— — — — — — — Broken line represents continuous communication and only selected, direct participation

◯ Coordinating bodies

▭ Personnel

ously, this was a technique to give attention to the goal-directed aspect of coordination. Such a clarification of philosophy and policy must be accomplished periodically by the top administration, if the second echelon is to identify appropriate interim goals and implement revisions or new programs needed to attain such interim and long-range goals.

The five staff members on the Task Force were the assistant superintendent, the high school principal, a junior high principal, an elementary principal, and chairman of a junior high social studies department. The continuing resource person for the group was a non-educator and resident of the school district experienced in long-range planning and forecasting.

Two products of this Task Force have given impetus and direction to many of the instructional improvements realized during subsequent years in our district. The first influential product was a restatement of district goals, part of which were the goals for the Ladue graduate and recommended ways to develop such a graduate.

The second significant product of the Task Force was a 1964 to 1970 long-range calendar of events to be accomplished in pursuit of the organizational goals, staff goals, content goals, method goals, and general goals. Such events were some of the recommended means for producing the ideal Ladue graduate.

Reproduced below from the Task Force Report are some sample goals and recommended 1968 targets for achieving those goals.

LONG-RANGE PROGRAM GOALS
FOR LADUE SCHOOL DISTRICT

ORGANIZATIONAL GOALS

1. Re-orient present organization structures and operating patterns now used for chronological age groupings to accommodate variable rates of individual pupil progress. . . .

1968

All secondary school course sequences and instruction to provide for flexible grouping and variable rates and limits of student progress.

Develop flexible class schedules in secondary schools to permit variable time allotments to subjects. . . .

STAFF GOALS

1. Continue and improve staff recruitment. . . .

1968

Remove legal obstacles and develop well-publicized policy of early teacher selection to include:

Granting future contracts to outstanding candidates contingent upon their successful completion of integrated university-Ladue program.

Providing initial salaries to provide appropriate incentives to early commitment (as above). . . .

CONTENT GOALS

1. Systematically reexamine entire curriculum. . . .

1968

Complete the re-evaluation of course sequences for elementary and secondary schools; make proposals for revision in light of content objectives and the program to develop skills of rational inquiry and logic. . . .

METHOD GOALS

1. Adopt revised methods of teaching and learning. . . .

1968

. . . Revise methods to insure improvements in developing inductive, deductive, analytical, categorization, and generalization skills.

Place in operation a formalized, recurring program of in-service methods workshops. . . .

The guideline here is: if a total system is to be goal-directed, then there must be some periodic procedure whereby over-all purposes are clarified and confirmed. Such a centrally conceived projection, in our case, required a centrally coordinated development and implementation. A quick backward glance at our official structure will convince you that we were appropriately organized for such an endeavor. It has been said, if power can do much evil, it is also true that without power not much good can be done.

The administrative council was in a position to initiate those actions suggested by the Task Force, as well as in a position to tailor to district-wide purposes any initiated action coming from building staffs, departments, or individual teachers.

Coordinating the revision of our K-12 visual arts program

All four aspects of effective coordination were well demonstrated by the six-year curriculum renewal effort by our visual arts staff. Goals were re-defined by the entire department. After goal-setting, the group cycled through planning and development, in-service and implementation, and the continuing phase of evaluation and recycling. Teams of from two to twenty cooperatively worked through the whole process, interacting with other departments, the business office, and the administrative councils whenever appropriate. And lastly, as the brief story which follows will show, the effort was very productive of curriculum materials and staff development.

In the first year, the high school art chairman led his teachers in examining to what extent their present classroom objectives and activities were appropriate for educating the variety of students enrolled, from the most talented to those having little sensitivity or interest in art.

Matters moved slowly that first and second year. By the third year the chairman was appointed Coordinator of Art for the entire district and the restructuring of the art curriculum began in earnest. Periodic meetings were held by the elementary and the secondary groups, with occasional meetings of the entire staff. By October of that third year, the preliminary draft of the revised elementary art guide began to emerge. The section on purpose and criteria was developed first.

As one small sample of the early work of that group, let me quote part of the criteria expressed by the Coordinator of Art.

CRITERION

Art should be evaluated in terms of what it does for each individual. Evaluation is concerned with the measurement of growth as evidenced by changes in behavior. Attention should be focused upon the behavior of a particular child in a particular situation as compared with his past behavior in other similar situations, rather than with the comparison of the performance of one child with another. . . .

With that good start, however, as often happens in actual situations, the process of deliberate, coordinated curriculum planning was interrupted for a time. The need for better facilities, better equipment, and the proper requisitioning of a greater variety of supplies demanded the major energies of the Coordinator of Art and his staff for the remainder of that third year and all of the fourth.

Nevertheless, the Art Coordinator was persistent. Beginning with the fifth year it was a different story. The Coordinator of Art made his master's degree project the involvement of all art staff in the development of "A Behaviorally Oriented Program of Visual Arts Education." In his over-all report on this project the Coordinator wrote:

The twenty art educators in the Ladue School District were integrally involved in the design of a behavioral sequential program of visual arts education for the Ladue Schools. Each staff member was given an opportunity to voice his opinions, feelings, and desires and to make suggestions about the art program through a survey. They shared their views in general and grade level workshops. . . .

The work sessions varied in length of time. There were three six-hour sessions (released time), three four-hour sessions (released time), and ten two-hour sessions (after school), plus many extra individual hours of homework.

Three attractive, detailed guides in Visual Arts Education in our district today provide ample evidence of the successful curriculum renewal project accomplished by our art staff under the effective leadership of our Coordinator of Visual Arts. However, the real benefits of this long effort can be best seen in the excitement and productivity of our youngsters as they and their teachers experience our behaviorally oriented art program, grades K-12.

In summary, then, it was the cooperative aspect of coordination that was well illustrated by the work of our Art Coordinator and staff. We might infer the following guidelines as explaining much of the success of that cooperative effort: considerable low-pressure time was provided for joint re-definition of goals; practical needs for better facilities and a greater variety of materials were met judiciously so that all teachers were directly enabled to do a more effective job; in-service training experiences were carefully planned to aid staff in the design and implementation of enriched visual arts learning environments; the progress of group planning was recorded in an agreed-upon format (see pp. 41-43) for easy sharing among the group; and common evaluation instruments and procedures were devised to measure the impact of the changes and to signal areas needing additional work.

Accountability and the processing of curriculum change

With your permission, I would like to step outside the curriculum change process for a moment and look at its significance in the context of the community and culture that sponsor it.

Emerging from the prolific curriculum changes of the 60's has been the very legitimate and logical question: How accountable are public schools to their patrons, the taxpayers, and to their consumers, the students? And a related question: How much are the schools in touch with the public they are supposed to serve?

Some obvious symptoms of the above doubts are the current rebellion of taxpayers and the unrest of students. School bureaucracies are being forced to face the fact that all to whom the school system must be accountable should be involved in defining the tasks it is to perform.

Like any dynamic entity in a changing environment, a school system, if it is to endure, must have an internal structure capable of performing the two basic functions of survival: maintenance and growth. This structure must possess both the power to hold to committed purposes and the flexibility to execute compensatory maneuvers for restoring orientation to a preselected course amidst changing environmental conditions. Obviously, such a structure must be sensitive to both the internal and external environments.

Our school system, like most, has been better organized for maintenance than for growth. While it has had intricate interlocking lines of authority and communication (see Figure 3-3) which keep the system preoccupied with the on-going conditions of its internal operations, it has had only a selected few lines of authority and communication keeping it responsive to the changing conditions of the external environment, and many of these are inactive a good part of the time.

When we look rather smugly at how well we are organized to develop and put new programs into operation, we must admit with some chagrin that all of this efficiency may well be misdirected if it is not germane to the needs of patrons and consumers that we are trying to serve. We must maintain our bearings in terms of the expectations of our patrons and the needs of our consumers. We must have open, active feedback from parents, taxpaying non-parents, and students.

One function of parents is to tell the school what they consider to be the most worthwhile attitudes, concepts, and skills that should be developed during the school years. And youngsters should be telling us what kinds of help they need to facilitate their acquisition of these worthwhile attitudes, concepts, and skills.

Most of the time the involvement of patrons and pupils looks something like the following: Taxpayers participate by voting in elections. Parents participate by attending the parent-teacher meetings and conferences. Youngsters participate by dutifully attending on schedule and performing with varied enthusiasm the prescribed exercises of the instructional program.

The tide seems to be turning and the waves of public protest are penetrating the sanctuaries of the public school. Patrons and pupils alike are saying that the powerful, gargantuan public school is not meeting their expectations and needs.

A simplistic description of their complaint is that there has been an overemphasis on academic, abstract learning at the expense of moral, emotional, and social growth. We have produced keen analyzers and articulate critics but have failed to cultivate youngsters with equal capacity to enjoy, to aspire, and to love. And the fully functioning human must be a reasonably balanced combination of all of these capacities and dispositions.

One passing thought is that some of the difficulty may lie in the fact that *form* should follow *function*. Large complex institutions take on incrusted forms that become unresponsive to the need for new functions. And the traditional form persists as an anachronism, supplying nonfunctional services in a population demanding more and different services. Exploding numbers, rising expectations, advanced technology, and depleted resources are some of the factors creating these new demands.

The larger picture, then, is that the public school must find a more functional relationship to the needs of the patrons and pupils it serves at the same time it increases the efficiency of its internal capacities to produce those needed services.

As the chart below indicates, teachers with the help of instructional specialists must perform their several social roles more responsibly by more nearly achieving an acceptable accountability to each group served.

Social roles of teachers	*Dimensions of accountability*
Member of school faculty (and professional associations)....	accountable to professional colleagues
Teacher of youngsters	accountable to individual and group of students
Employee of taxpayers	accountable to parents and non-parents
Carriers of culture....................	accountable to past and present scholars and artists
Specialists in a coordinated school district enterprise...........	accountable to immediate superior officer in the institution

Utilizing shared leadership and shifting roles of students, parents, lay specialists, teachers, administrators, and coordinators

Our best effort to attend to all these dimensions of accountability was most evident in the recent revision of our sex education program, grades K-12. Also demonstrated by that sex education project was the complexity that evolves as school staff and lay persons wrestle jointly with the goal-setting, cyclical, cooperative, and productive aspects of curriculum planning. What had to be found was a proper distribution and assignment of staff, students, parents, and lay resource persons over all of the four aspects of the curriculum renewal process.

Beginning with an all-day workshop in February a few years ago, we involved persons from all five groups to whom we felt accountable, namely, special scholars in the field (gynecologists and religious leaders), parents in the district, administrators, teachers, and students. Representatives from the first four groups participated in the lecture and discussion groups of the workshop. Students were involved on subsequent occasions as they helped evaluate printed material and audio-visual aids, or submitted to teachers the questions they wanted answered about sex.

Workshop participants, both lay and professional, professed that the lectures and discussions were helpful personally. Nevertheless, they made no specific suggestions about changes to be made in the instructional program. Probably the most we accomplished in that particular conference was an increased readiness for a new effort to update and revitalize our local sex education program under the direction of the Health and Sex Education Steering Committee appointed earlier that year by the Administrative Council.

(See Figure 3-4.)

Taking the chart as our reference, let me report as succinctly as possible the roles played by different groups during the two-and-a-half years of that school-community effort to revitalize our sex education program.

To: Administrative Council

From: Coordinator of Instruction

Re: Organizational Proposal for Coordination, Production, and Evaluation of Sex Education Program, K-12.

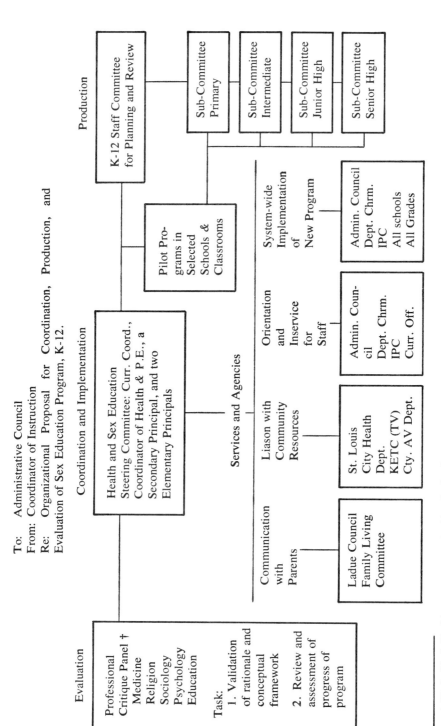

† We had individual lay persons serve in this role, but have not organized them as a panel.

Figure 3-4. Organizational Proposal for Coordination, Production, and Evaluation of Sex Education Program, K-12

March, April, and May of the first year:

The Sex Education Steering Committee surveyed the staffs of individual buildings for any evidence of impact that the workshop may have had, and for implications of next steps.

The principals reacted with divided opinions about whether changes were needed in the sex education program. However, the steering committee, knowing the expressed interest of many parents, did not allow the matter to be dropped.

The steering committee met again and formulated an organizational chart (see Figure 3-4) of lay and professional groups who would be responsible for the re-examination and ultimate revision of the sex education program, K-12. The strategy here was to establish a "form" which the more motivated steering committee felt would "function" cooperatively to marshall all appropriate resources in a sound revision of our program.

The *elementary principals reviewed and approved* the organizational chart and proposed procedures. They also approved appointments of teachers to the Sex Education Staff Planning Committee.

The sixteen-member Sex Education Staff Planning Committee heard reports of present instructional programs and recommendations regarding what teachers felt needed to be done to improve the program. The Coordinators of Instruction and the Coordinator of Health submitted a joint statement containing a proposed "Rationale for Sex Education Program," and a scope and sequence chart of the topics, activities, materials, and staff deployment of the then current program.

September to December of the first year:

News reports and special literature from anti-sex education groups such as the Christian Crusade began to put a damper on both staff and parental interest in an expanded sex education program.

With a new school year, the Sex Education K-12 Staff Planning Committee reviewed the diversity and optional nature of the present program, this review being done for the special benefit of new committee members. The one common interest of this group of teachers seemed to be in locating new materials for parents, teachers, and students.

During this month the Coordinator of Instruction and the Coordinator of Health drafted a proposal for the selection of audio-visual materials to carry the "core" of basic information we wanted students to have on sexuality, human reproduction, personal development, and inter-personal relationships.

The Administrative Council (elementary and secondary principals) approved the proposal of the Sex Education Steering Committee to search for audio-visual materials.

As per the above plan, the Sex Education Staff Planning Committee previewed twenty-five films and sound filmstrips on a day of released time.

Members of Ladue Council Family Living Committee and elementary principals jointly evaluated and approved seven of the ten audio-visual aids recommended by the Staff Planning Committee.

Progress during the second year and third year:

The Staff Planning Committee planned an in-service day for viewing of approved audio-visual materials by multi-graded groups of teachers, to assure their knowledge of materials to be used in their grade plus those used by the next two lower grades.

A special film, *Parent to Child*, and an overview of our revised sex education program were presented to the total Ladue District Council, consisting of the president and three representatives from each parent-teacher association in our district, all principals, the superintendent, and his assistant.

Elementary principals devoted most of an afternoon meeting to a discussion of the success of our implementation of the program, particularly in the face of a national climate very antagonistic to any such programs. They decided that "the program was on firm ground because of parent involvement in its development."

The Sex Education Steering Committee met to review progress and project plans for review of secondary materials by staff and parents.

Secondary parents, secondary principals, and physical education and homemaking teachers reviewed and selected materials on sex education to be used in grades 7-12. This meeting lasted five hours.

Elementary principals discussed the outline of a proposed guide on the use of audio-visual materials in sex education, K-6. During the next month, parents assisted teachers in observing and assessing students' reactions to some new filmstrips with sound. The guide was produced and distributed to teachers.

With continuing support of the parents and with the Instructional Planning Center circulating the carefully selected audio-visual materials to be seen by all students, the sex education program, at least for the moment, arrived at a high point of renewal and impact. Accountability seemed to have been discharged to students, parents, taxpayers, fellow teachers, administrators, and scholars in the field.

One closing remark about the various roles of the building principal is in order at this point. It is clear in the foregoing report that the principal played a crucial role in program development. What was not so clear was his key role in the implementation. He did at least two things. Typically, during the fall, the building principal arranged one or more meetings for parents to view and discuss the sex education materials which their youngsters would see. Also, throughout the year the principal assisted his teachers in identifying the most appropriate times to incorporate those studies into the on-going instructional program at each level. If the principal fell down in either of those roles, the probability of actual implementation of a sex education program in any given building decreased markedly.

Legitimizing in-service work as an integral part of the regular school calendar

The closing sections of this chapter will highlight some factors most influential in the production of people-growth and program development, the fourth functional aspect of the coordination and nurture of planning teams. In a general way, we will be talking about the requisite conditions for professionalizing the whole business of staff development and curriculum improvement.

The form of the school calendar for the professional staff fits the teaching function, but it totally ignores the function of professional growth and curriculum improvement. Many of the nonprofessional staff work the year around, using the time when the students are away as an opportunity to renovate and recondition facilities and equipment. The day should not be far off when the professional staff will be employed year-round to discharge properly its multiple functions of program design, development, implementation, and evaluation.

One of the main concerns, if not *the* main concern of the instructional coordinators when they meet regularly in our central office, is the problem of how to make in-service growth a legitimate part of the regular assignment of the practicing educator, be he classroom teacher, principal, counselor, coordinator, or superintendent. Given not only the usual constraints of limited time, space, and energy, but also the insistent demands of current operations, we find the problem almost insoluble. When we take seriously the need for continual in-service growth, the time and attention given to it is abysmally inadequate. We continue to live the frustration of trying to accomplish an important job with subminimal conditions and little likelihood of total success.

When partial success is realized in a given time and place (such as instances reported in this book), it has to be considered a miracle totally unpredictable on the basis of prevailing conditions. It can be accounted for only by the fact that several staff members have gone the second and third mile beyond their official commitment to the school district. However, piling developmental tasks on top of a full teaching load takes its toll somewhere. Even the seemingly best arrangements, namely, releasing of teachers, deprives the learning environment of its prime ingredient, the affectionate, experienced, and knowledgeable adult counselor. And in so doing we charge to the student the real cost to upgrade program and staff.

Twelve months' employment with only nine months of classes makes sense to persons who have a proper appreciation of what teachers have to do to make those nine months of classes optimum learning environments for youngsters. Given twelve months' employment, two to four weeks of paid vacation, and nine months of teaching, there would be a remaining period of eight to ten weeks when teachers and administrators could be working on professional development and the production of instructional plans and materials. The exploding array of new materials and techniques, the continuing trend toward the personal service aspects of the teacher's role, the crescendo of the patron's and pupil's cry for relevance, lead me to conclude that planned, paid-for allotted time for in-service will become more and more justified with each passing year. The advent of the packaged curriculum has not lessened the teacher's role as the final decision-maker in adapting learning materials and environments to the needs of specific learners. Chapter Four describes instances of how this happens in today's classroom. In fact, one main thesis of this book is the necessity of increased staff involvement in all levels of curriculum planning and instructional improvement.

The Assistant Coordinator of Instruction at one of our monthly coordinators' meetings made the suggestion that we classify staff meetings according to two quite different types. In a general way he would classify them according to Bloom's taxonomy of cognitive skills.

One type would be the "sharing" type, where knowledge and comprehension of knowledge about content and methods would be exchanged among members of a staff on a building, grade level, or departmental basis. Such meetings have been found very necessary for the effective implementation and coordination of the "established" curriculum. The "sharing"-type meeting makes modest demands upon the practitioner, since the task is either to report a practice in which the reporter is presently engaged, or to comprehend a report by some colleague or visiting expert. Little, if any, other kinds of behavior are expected. Obviously, such meetings make only incidental contributions to either curriculum revision or professional growth.

The second type of meeting would be of an "in-service" type where application, analysis, synthesis, and evaluation of content and methods were to be dealt with. In such meetings it would be expected that something would happen to cause the practitioner to acquire new skills, different perspective, up-dated facts and theories, or deeper insight into self and relations with others. Out of such efforts might well come some visible new frame of reference and revised instructional plans. Without a doubt these kinds of interaction place considerably more demands upon the participants.

However, by the same token, they are the types of experience which have the highest potential for bringing about changes in the behavior of the practitioner, and consequently, real changes in the learning environment of youngsters.

Perhaps another way to view these two types, as alluded to in the beginning of this chapter, is to think of type I as a dealing with "form" and type II as a redefining of "function." Let it be reiterated that a fundamental revision of functions is the only sound base for designing new forms that persist because they do in fact implement the new functions.

A quick look at our calendar of in-service will show how we allocate time for the two types of meetings just described.

We begin each fall with a Pre-session Week, five days of preparation before classes begin. Monday of that week is split, morning for total staff general sessions and afternoon for separate building staff organizational sessions under the building principals. Included, or course, are special orientation conferences for new staff members, relying heavily on a "sponsoring teacher" buddy system. Most, if not all, of these first day sessions could be classified as type I, mainly dealing with administrative routine. The occasional exception is the use of one hour for an inspirational speech that launches the theme for the in-service of the next two days, such as was the case of the Pre-session Week on behavioral objectives reported in Chapter One.

Tuesday and Wednesday of Pre-session Week usually consists of grade level, departmental, and building meetings organized around a combination of type II work sessions on a theme, or type I exchanges readying each group for the coming school year. We have learned that anything beyond five hours devoted to application, analysis, synthesis, and evaluation is more than staff can bear during this week, when their main concern is getting themselves, their classrooms, and resources in top readiness for the influx of students.

Quite regularly, the grade level and departmental sessions do involve teachers in analysis and practice exercises which will prepare them for more skillful use of new curriculums recently developed and/or adopted by the district. For instance, in August 1970 all intermediate teachers had a full day's training on the Lippitt and

Fox *Social Science Laboratory Units*, while eighth grade teachers analyzed and evaluated Harvard Social Studies training films in preparation for implementing Ladue's eighth grade American Issues course, developed and published locally, incorporating the use of selected AEP pamphlets.

Thursday and Friday of Pre-session Week find staffs in their own buildings working individually, in small groups and/or as a building staff, making final preparations for the opening of classes.

In summary then, it appears that one day out of five during Pre-session Week is devoted to type II in-service of an instructional nature while the rest of the time is used for type I cooperative planning or individual preparation of classrooms. Any heavier dose of in-service has been resented by staff, claiming that it deprived them of adequate time for preparing their materials and classrooms. However, it can also be shown that impressions made during the Pre-session Week do transfer into the year's planning and procedures. Such was the case when behavioral objectives and classroom management skills were emphasized.

As was implied earlier, Pre-session ought to involve full employment during the entire month of August, with three weeks for type II sessions on curriculum development and human relations training, plus the fourth week devoted to classroom preparation. We would then have the best of both requisite conditions for a successful launching of instructional programs—a charged-up teacher, and a thoroughly prepared learning environment.

Once we are into the year, we declare the third week of every month as reserved for after-school, district-wide grade level and departmental meetings. Such accommodations permit both horizontal and vertical coordination as needed. By special arrangements through the administrative councils, clearance and/or released time can be secured for in-school-hour interschool or out-of-district visitations. Also, ''extended'' late afternoon or evening buffet sessions can be set up for groups who need a longer time-block. Such sessions as these were part of the formats used by the sex education committee reported earlier in this chapter. The one-hour afternoon meetings by necessity are type I sharing sessions, whereas the extended afternoon and evening buffets can accommodate effective type II work sessions.

The last day of the first semester is declared an in-service day. Secondary teachers use this day for administratively closing out one semester and preparing for the next. Elementary staff are usually involved in some type II groups treating some aspect of the one or two curriculum areas under intensive examination and redevelopment at that time. For example, most recently our total elementary staff devoted a one-day, end-of-semester workshop to "Alternatives to the Self-Contained Classroom."

Another in-service day is usually declared in association with the weekend of Washington's Birthday. At this time in the school year, both secondary and elementary staff on a district-wide basis can crystallize some important curriculum decisions which set the framework for the developmental and productive work to be accomplished during the spring and the summer. It is during this time and the remaining months of the school year that all of the preliminary investigations and preparations are made for the many IPC summer projects, like those described at the end of Chapter Two.

Chapter Six gives a complete description of the organization and procedures of the Instructional Planning Center. At this point, however, it should be said that summer task forces receive one to five days of released time during the spring to do preliminary work on their approved summer projects. Between March and June they can still involve all other appropriate staff members in their deliberations. These arrangements of preliminary involvement assure the effective transfer of tasks from one group to another, as pointed out in the beginning of this chapter. Once the summer arrives, they are on their own until they report back to the larger group during the Pre-session Week. As already indicated in Chapter Two, summer production committees work from one to six weeks between June and August. These sessions are type II, applying and synthesizing knowledge with some critical excursions into analysis and evaluation diagrammed on the flow chart for summer teams, pp. 44-48.

Summarizing the formally scheduled district-wide accommodations for type I and type II instructional planning sessions is not enough. The total picture is not complete until we acknowledge the inestimable amount of instructional decision-making that is generated and guided by principals, counselors, department heads, grade level conveners, and teachers at each individual building. Such day-by-day, week-by-week continuous planning accounts for most of the effective maintenance and renewal of our instructional programs. Some appreciation of these efforts can be gained by reading the descriptions of small and large curriculum improvements reported in Chapter Four.

Communicating inside and outside

Functional communication within the school district and between the school staff and the outside world is the sine qua non of effective curriculum planning. It is equally important to the smooth operation of the school. There are at least four types of items to be communicated: policies, operational procedures, progress reports on research and development, and news reports of successful programs, events, practices, and the persons involved.

Communication is both oral and written. The oral exchange occurs at meetings of groups listed earlier, namely, the Board of Education (once a month), the joint elementary-secondary administrative council (five or six times a year), the secondary administrators (twice a month), the elementary administrators (twice a month), the instructional coordinators (once a month), the high school instructional council (twice a month), secondary departments (once a month), elementary grade groups (once a month), and individual building staffs (once a month or more). Other ad hoc groups meet at a frequency required to get the job done. Innumerable individual and small group conferences and telephone conversations augment this entire oral communication system, filling in gaps, clarifying intents, and soothing bruised feelings.

Visible and stable form is given to the oral exchange by a parallel network of written communication. Handbooks and memoranda undergird the understanding of policies and procedures. For example, some time ago the instructional division distributed a policy memo regarding the finding of time for instructional improvement. Because of its general relevance to the whole problem of coordination, part of that memo is printed at the close of this chapter.

Progress reports of departmental and grade level groups are distributed to all administrators and coordinators as well as to all teachers involved in each group. The INTER-COM (central office memo) is published about twice a week by one or more of the instructional coordinators, giving recognition to successful practices and events, or announcing special optional in-service opportunities coming in the next week or so.

Our Director of Public Relations publishes an eight- to sixteen-page *Bulletin* that is mailed once a month to all residents in the school district. News releases also go to local mass media, either promoted by us or solicited by them.

Administrators, counselors, and coordinators engage whenever necessary in direct communication with school patrons through the mail, by phone, by conference, and at parent-teacher meetings. All principals and four representatives from each parent-teacher association meet six times a year as the Ladue School District Council to foster the flow of information between the school and the community, and to cooperatively sponsor such enterprises as adult education, bussing, summer school, and recreation. Reports of major efforts in curriculum change are presented periodically to the district council.

Reporting "up" and feeding "down"

It is the two-way nature of inside communication that will be briefly discussed in this section. It is probably safe to say that all institutions develop active channels for dispensing information, but few have an effective grassroots feedback system, at least one that exerts full-fledged corrective influence on its operations. And the typical school system may be an exemplary model of this deficiency.

In school districts it is difficult for teachers to be heard beyond their school building or for students to be heard beyond the classroom. In both cases their influence is metered through many screens before it begins to affect decisions regarding the basic functions and forms of the total district.

The tenor of our times has school leaders searching for ways to open the two-way flow of ideas between the teachers and the central office. This seems to have been helped in our district by establishing the Instructional Planning Center and Professional Library, both of which offer useful services and resources to teachers. The flow of teachers to and from the central office has steadily increased. We are finding that the expanded, coordinated 7-12th grade journalism program has the potential for amplifying the student's voice, but only time will tell. We also hope that the expanded, direct involvement of students in instructional planning and production may turn out to be the most appropriate and effective way for their influence to be felt. A few instances of this sort are scattered throughout the reports in this book, but they are admittedly too sparse. See the Index for "student's role."

Finding time for instructional improvement

As an appropriate close of this chapter on communication and the coordination of curriculum planning teams, let me reprint in part a memo of a few years back which attempted to clarify the central office policy regarding time for instructional improvement.

Some guidelines for judicious use of time for curriculum change and staff development.

1. Extended afternoon sessions or released time arrangements should be reserved for *those types of curriculum tasks* which by their very nature require 1½ to 4 hours of group interaction in a special situation using special resource people and special instructional materials and equipment. Three such types of tasks are:
   a) Developing goals and conceptual framework for curriculum changes,
   b) Holding training sessions for learning new teaching techniques, and
   c) Having sessions for disseminating new methods and materials from pilot teachers to total grade level or department.

2. Other curriculum office tasks such as (a) exhibiting and circulating new instructional materials, (b) coordinating the implementation of new programs, and (c) evaluating the effect of new programs will be done totally by the Coordinators and IPC staff during the regular school day or at ½ to 1 hour after-school meetings when the teaching staff needs to be involved.

3. A total committee, grade group, or department (10-30 persons) should each be released separately at that particular time when its job needs to be done and when the special resources can be arranged to assist it in accomplishing its job. When this is impossible, a half day of in-service for either the elementary and/or secondary schools might be declared and the tasks of the several groups scheduled to the date of such an in-service session.

4. Projects involving long-range, complex development of new instructional programs should be researched, carefully defined and planned during the school year. Appropriate task force groups should be employed during the summer for the actual production of methods and materials.

5. Training of teachers in extensive, new content and teaching techniques should be scheduled either in a series of weekly evening meetings or for one or two weeks in the summer (with pay) to provide adequate time accessible to the greatest number of participants.

6. Time spent on graduate studies can be incorporated into in-service efforts by arranging appropriate courses and workshops with credit and staff provided by cooperating colleges and universities.

Recommended limits on use of time for curriculum change and staff development.

For the individual teacher:

1. The maximum released time (taken out of a classroom) for any individual teacher during the school year for *work on central office-sponsored curriculum improvement* should be 2 days or four ½ days.

2. Usually no teacher should be asked to participate in more than one district-wide curriculum committee.

3. The fact of prior commitments to administrative committees, professional association responsibilities, individual building responsibilities, or university-related assignments should be considered when assigning teachers to membership on curriculum planning committees.

4. Membership of district-wide curriculum committees will be selected from a list of candidates recommended by the principals.

5. The curriculum office periodically will make a survey of the total staff to determine participation in curriculum planning committees, administrative committees, professional associations, individual

buildings, and university-related assignments.

a) To insure that generally no teacher's classroom instruction time is disrupted more than 2 full days per year due to released time for curriculum work, and

b) To attempt to involve as many different staff members as possible in curriculum work.

6. One or two projects by individual teachers should be approved each year as special, summer assignments.

7. Release of teachers requested by out-of-district agencies (e.g. Universities) should be cleared through the administrators and the curriculum office.

FOUR

Harvesting curriculum renewal in the classroom, the school, and the district

The first problem in harvesting anything is to know what that thing is. Or, as my farming father used to say, "I don't want you weeding the celery beds until you know the difference between young celery plants and weeds."

How does one identify a genuine instance of curriculum renewal? What's the size and shape of a quality crop? What are the criterion characteristics of a quality version of curriculum improvement?

This chapter is designed to answer the above questions. Therefore, it will consist primarily of descriptions of the many sizes and shapes of curriculum renewal. And secondly, it will employ one kind of analysis that can be used to judge the authenticity and apparent impact of different kinds of curriculum changes on the environment of learners in a public school system.

Defining curriculum renewal

Allow me to remind you that on page 17 we defined curriculum as the "never-ending invention of learning environments." We also said that such invention "is a social process," and that "learning environments consist of *persons, things,* and *activities* organized to foster the developmental fulfillment and desired behavioral patterns of all learners, young and old."

Now then, to the above definitions let us add one for curriculum renewal. An important use of this criterion definition is to evaluate the quality of any accomplished curriculum change.

Curriculum renewal is the *end product* of curriculum inventing and implementing. Specifically, it is *changes in persons, things,* and *activities* that are (1) *better addressed to eliciting some desired change in the learner,* (2) *more validly selected or developed to enable the learner to make the change,* (3) *more efficient and humane means for communication among all persons involved,* (4) *more positive and immediate feedback to the learner of progress he is making,* and (5) *more broadly and soundly supported resources to meet the continuing demands of new groups parading through such learning environments.*

Authenticating all sizes and shapes of curriculum renewal

There are two basic dimensions by which curriculum renewal can be described besides the five criterion characteristics defined above. I am thinking of geographic and chronological dimensions, different *modules of space and time* by which we can describe and classify any curriculum change effort. Any specific effort should be describable both in terms of the size of the life-space (arena) in which the curriculum inventors are operating and in terms of the time consumed.

The picture I shall paint in this chapter displays curriculum renewal as occurring in the classroom (Arena One), the school (Arena Two), and the district (Arena Three) over a range of time modules as short as a teacher's lesson and as long as a decade, from beginning to end of a district-wide curriculum revision.

In Arena One we have the teacher and students in a given classroom. For the most part, all are mutually and directly involved in the target learning environment. Input of verbal and nonverbal ideas contributed by students and the teacher are the substance of the curriculum change occurring in that room. For as the learning experience develops, so goes the curriculum change. I would suggest that we apply the criterion characteristics from our definition of quality curriculum renewal if we seek to establish the significance of the change made by the teacher. Nevertheless, despite the degree of significance, in my view even the least of these changes is *very* authentic since it possesses a direct relationship to what is happening to individual learners. This is not always true of the acts in Arenas Two and Three.

In Arena Two (the school) we have the teacher, principal, other teachers, occasionally a few students, and perhaps some parents. These persons are engaged in revising activities on the basis of past learning experiences or projecting curricular plans in terms of the immediately upcoming classroom sessions. It can be expected that such deliberations have a slightly less direct bearing on the responses of the students. However, they do carry considerable potential for influencing future encounters. As such, I judge them to be very authentic performances in the circus of curriculum improvement.

Finally, in Arena Three we have the principals, curriculum supervisors, central office administrators, a lay board of education, with on-call appearances of teachers, unsolicited intrusions by an occasional parent (usually by letter) and/or student. Of course, hovering around this third arena and frequently penetrating the second are such persons as commercial representatives, local university personnel, state and federal agents, as well as official and unofficial *ad hoc* community groups.

It becomes an absorbing puzzle when one attempts to contemplate how all of these persons actually influence the curriculum. As I write this note, I am aware that tomorrow morning a sizable group of central office personnel will analyze a patron's threatening letter condemning two student-written editorials about the war moratorium. The ultimate effect of this missile may be substantial curriculum changes in our journalism program as it moves from Arena Three, through Arena Two, to Arena One.

Perhaps the one current geographic concept I might reinforce with this book is that *continuous curriculum renewal is a cluster of interdependent activities (supporting or conflicting) occurring in the classroom, the school, and the school system, including the community at large*. It's a three-ring arrangement. However, unlike a circus, they are three *concentric rings* with actors moving somewhat freely from one arena to another. The acts in each are equally authentic—be it a classroom teacher deciding whether to answer a child's question about human sexuality or referring it to the home (a curriculum decision), be it an individual school debating how it will involve the parents in an exchange about what and how to teach their children about sexual development and behavior, or be it a district-wide steering committee struggling with the basic question of how to incorporate human sexuality into the larger curriculum of human growth and development.

I never cease to be intrigued by the process by which acts in Arena Three send ripples into the other rings. For instance, it is exciting to trace how a new social studies program, begun from a rationale developed in Arena Three, given a predetermined form in Arena Two, will touch and elicit from learners in Arena One some desired response consistent with the original rationale. Many persons are still very dubious that it can really happen that way. Our experience says it can, the whole process being one continuous flow of events from rationale to student response.

Asking questions to analyze the quality of curriculum renewal

In the remainder of this chapter we will describe a great many instances of successful curriculum renewal. In each case we will apply some analytical questions to determine the extent to which the renewal *reflected our five criterion characteristics of genuine curriculum improvement*. Obviously, these questions should be useful in guiding the development of effective curriculum change, as well as in evaluating the quality of the accomplished change. Remember, the substance of curriculum renewal lies in the *changes in persons, things, and activities* deliberately instituted in a learning environment. In other words, if there are significant changes in content and method, they will have been inserted into the new learning environment through detectable, describable changes in the persons, things, and activities which constitute that new learning environment.

A *first quality check* is an explicit examination of the changes in purposes of the persons involved in the teaching-learning situation. What new decisions were made about the behavioral changes to be elicited in the learners? What were the behavioral objectives for the learners? How did these expected student performances relate to existing expectations of the school and the community? How did they relate to the assumed needs and interests (developmental stage) of the learners? And how did they relate to their previous training and experience?

A *second check for quality* in a curriculum change is to evaluate the experience and research which led to the introduction of revised methods and materials *which were to enable learners to achieve* an expected behavioral chenage. What experience and scholarship guided the selection of the ideas and skills which were to bring about the desired changes in the learners' capacities and dispositions? On the basis of what theory and experimental studies did the designers select and incorporate the modes of interaction (climate, roles, and relationships) through which learners would confront these concepts and skills?

A *third quality check* is inexorably tied to the second, for it has to do with the particular communication media selected to aid the learners in their confrontation with essential concepts and skills. Such media run the gamut *from* objects to be manipulated, events to be dramatized, and persons to be interviewed, *to* simulations, games, pictures, films, tapes, books, chalk, and talk.

Typical questions to be answered in this third check are: What means of communication in what social settings would enable students to achieve the objectives? How well were basic concepts displayed and explained? How well were basic skills demonstrated? And what interesting variety of media, methods, and materials was employed for the enjoyable, effective acquisition of the selected ideas and skills?

A *fourth quality check* has to do with feedback. What system existed to signal periodically (if not automatically) the positive effect of the curriculum revision for bringing about the desired changes in student performance? (See the seventh grade mathematics project described in Chapter Seven.) Were the evaluation criteria and devices consistent with the original instructional objectives? And to what extent were the learners and teachers informed of the criteria upon which progress was to be judged?

A *fifth quality check* has to do with the maintenance of support for a given curriculum change. What forces and paraphernalia will exist to maintain an accomplished change? After the first run of the revised curriculum, what remains to insure that it can be effectively repeated the next time it falls on the calendar? How will it adjust to different groups of learners? What will happen if the teacher is new? And will the in-puts become inappropriate, unavailable, or obsolete? What about continuing costs?

Now, let us start with Arena One and describe, from the simplest to the most complex, the variety of modules of curriculum improvement produced in our current situation. Note the varying time sequences of the several projects.

Executing the "active" phase of curriculum renewal in Arena One

One fall, a pilot teacher of one of our locally-produced sixth grade social studies units found the students "bogged down," at least in terms of the pre-set objective of the latter part of that unit. The total unit was centered on the idea of social order and was pointed toward having students induce some hypotheses about what physical, social, and psychological factors contribute to the establishment and maintenance of social order.

In this particular section, students were given pictures, news stories, and tables of demographic data from which they were (1) to draw inferences about the general living conditions in a large urban ten-year-old housing development, and (2) to formulate hypotheses about what factors might be contributing to such conditions.

The pictures and statistics made it quite clear to students that conditions were bad. The crime, the filth, the destruction, and the deterioration were very visible. But students needed help in seeing some of the less visible personal and social factors which were missing and possibly whose absence was contributing to these bad living conditions.

Demonstrating considerable sensitivity to the students' difficulty as well as good insight into the whole idea of social order, this teacher asked the class: "What were some of the failures in responsibilities on the part of the planners, builders, managers, and tenants?" And also, "What was missing in this housing project, both physical and *nonphysical*?"

These questions elicited a flood of student responses which the teacher charted on the board, including the following:

What Is Missing in This Housing Project?

Physical	Nonphysical
1. Jobs	1. Sympathy for children
2. Clinic	2. Teaching right from wrong
3. More police	3. Nursery care
4. Recreation area for adults	4. Supervised play
5. Shopping center	5. Respect for building
6. School nearby	6. No love or concern for anybody
7. Family care	7. More self-discipline
8. Adequate street lights	8. Basic missing ingredient: No system of government for a "city" of 10,000 people

The final "nonphysical" item presaged the formation of a self-governing social structure which, one year after that classroom episode, was officially recognized by city officials as the St. Louis Civic Alliance for Housing.

However, the real point is that a masterful teacher had on-the-spot devised a learning environment which enabled sixth graders to hypothesize that responsible involvement might be a potent force in establishing and maintaining social order. Needless to say, the charts developed by the students working with this pilot teacher were included in the revised teacher's guide to suggest a specific technique, if needed, to assist other groups toward a similar insight.

As to my analysis of the substance of this curriculum-improvement event, I would point up the following: (1) the teacher was keenly aware of the student response expected at this point and the important relationship of that response to the goal of the entire unit, (2) the teacher identified correctly the kind of bridge the students needed to associate the conditions they perceived and the possible factors contributing to those conditions; for example, a needed sense of responsibile involvement on the part of tenants, (3) the teacher formulated the right questions to elicit relevant responses from the students, and (4) the teacher displayed the student responses in a chart form which aided the students in associating conditions with possible causes, thereby permitting the students to realize that they had successfully achieved a reasonable closure on the main objective of the lesson.

I hope that the above report serves as an explicit illustration of the "active" curriculum building which happens every day in Arena One of the master teacher.

A second instance of this type of individual curriculum planning has a more extended and complex history. It began with a teacher's "cranking out" vocabulary worksheets once a week and ended with his contract for the publication of a tenth grade vocabulary workbook. This was to be the first of several commercially published texts by this young man. Printed below are excerpts from his IPC proposal.

> The vocabulary program would consist of a series of approximately 125 daily lessons, each of which introduces two new words (or word stems or prefixes) and requires the student to work through several types of exercises using both the new words and previously introduced words. (See sample attached.) The lessons would be bound into a workbook, along with appropriate enrichment materials, such as crossword puzzles using the vocabulary words.
>
> In addition, bi-weekly quizzes and quarter and semester examinations would be prepared, but would not be bound. All materials would be mimeographed so that additional copies could be produced easily and inexpensively at the high school.

Obviously, these learning activities were relevant to the curricular context and developmental level of the target students. In fact, the teacher reported that:

> During the school year 1966-1967, I produced an experimental set of vocabulary materials designed to correct some of the shortcom-

ings of existing materials, and used them with some one hundred tenth-grade English students, with significant success, measured both in terms of achievement on examinations and responses from students (many of whom felt this was the first method of vocabulary study to be of significant help to them), as well as spontaneous use of the new words in speech and compositions. Other teachers—at both the tenth-grade and other levels—have expressed interest in adopting the new materials for the school year 1967-1968.

Since the commercially published edition of these instructional materials is being used by us and many other high schools, I can happily note that this curriculum change launched in Arena One of a single high school teacher has sent ripples through similar arenas spread spottily across the national market.

Particularly worthy of note for our purposes is the dual base, educational research and classroom experience, which this teacher used in building his specifications for this instructional improvement. With careful planning he related the student objectives to the larger curricular context and the interest level of students. Having once hooked the student, the teacher led him to an exercise of "higher order intellectual skills" and did not merely occupy his time in some inane, repetitive task. Since papers were corrected in class, students received immediate feedback about their correct or incorrect understanding of the words in each lesson.

Processing deliberately planned curriculum change in six months or less time

The next size module of curriculum change above a single teacher's effort is a cooperative project of two teachers. This is still an Arena One operation, except that a second teacher enters as a resource person. An exemplary instance of this kind was reported to me by the Language Arts Coordinator who previously taught English as a member of a 7th grade interdisciplinary teaching team. His cooperative planning and teaching with a resource teacher extended from December through March, a 4-month module. The story is best told in his own words.

> Observing their success (with small scale creative writing under a student teacher), I became convinced of the need for and value of a *more formal encounter with creative writing.*

In this manner, our 7th grade English teacher framed the general instructional objective for this special project. Now, for our first quality check, note how he proceeded to relate this learning experience to the pre-existing curriculum as well as to the developmental stage, previous training, and experience of this combined group of one hundred 7th graders.

> I asked Mrs.————————, the sponsor of the creative writing club, to help me structure a creative writing experience. I was not willing, however, simply to relinquish to her responsibility for the task. Together we worked out a plan for an articulated project and began to refine it. I turned over to her my ditto file of the previous and current year's assignments. At the same time I gave her six or seven student files which contained papers written for each assignment.
> Later, when she had read these materials, she visited my class to observe small group discussion in which students were reading and evaluating their own papers written as responses to selected short stories.

Please hear next the careful plans made both to motivate good effort and to assist each student toward a performance of high quality.

> With that background, we decided that a twenty-minute introduction to the topic of creative writing via pieces by seventh graders published in *Tusitala,* [the school's] creative writing publication, during the past five years would be a powerful and encouraging stimulus.

As per our second quality check, it can be reported that "model" pieces selected for the sampler demonstrated such qualities as simplicity, vivid imagery, precise diction, and common figures of speech. Note the comprehensive analysis and the effective use of audio-visuals and guest students in the presentation by the resource teacher.

On the day of her presentation, Mrs.——distributed the sampler, projected on the screen her choice for analysis. . . . At the conclusion of her analysis, Mrs.——introduced three of her creative writing club members who read one of their own recent works and commented on it. As far as my students were concerned, it had been a pleasant guest lecture situation. We initiated no other follow-up at this point.

About two weeks later, Mrs.——returned to make an assignment. On this visit, she assumed the role of teacher rather than featured speaker. In a fifteen-minute presentation she set up the experience.

The use of three guest students and the shifting of her own roles were exemplary media for displaying the concepts and skills to be acquired.

Student production was nurtured along as follows:

Students spent the next thirty minutes writing their first drafts. . . . the next day the writers met in small groups to share their writing and react to that of others. . . . they produced their second drafts in a period of thirty-five to forty minutes. . . .

Three days after the students had handed in their papers, Mrs.——returned to our classroom. She brought all the marked papers, a selection of eight for in-depth analysis, and a very favorable reaction to their writing.

Then came the final effort and publication, ultimately, for several pieces.

The students rewrote their papers a week later in an attempt to improve them as Mrs.————had indicated. . . . As the time approached for the annual publication of *Tusitala*, the number of pieces for publication which grew out of this project was high. . . .

And the teacher's closing remark was: "I look upon this project as one of the most successful of my career as a seventh grade teacher."

Putting in my own last word, I wish to point out the forces and paraphernalia that exist in the situation to help maintain and

even disseminate this fine example of curriculum improvement.
I shall mention only those that seem most important. First, the
staff organization remains, namely, an interdisciplinary team and
an available resource teacher. Second, a Language Arts Coordinator
is now around to suggest the involvement of this special composition
teacher in other subject areas as well as English. And third, the
realistic and influential target of published writings in the *Tusitala*
is still there. These factors should cause the continuation of this
practice.

An equally interesting but quite different kind of deliberate
restructuring of the learning environment was the Labor-
Management-Government Simulation Game, developed and
executed cooperatively by three junior high social studies teachers
and one student teacher. This project was launched about a year
ago as a way of augmenting a locally-created eighth grade unit
entitled "Unresolved Problems in Income Distribution."

A project such as this had sufficient carryover to the homes
that the principal kept himself well-informed of its development
and execution. Therefore, it is properly categorized as an Arena
Two curricular event within a pre-set context from Arena Three,
namely, the district-wide experimental eighth grade social studies
project sponsored by the Instructional Planning Center during
two recent summer periods.

In order to properly create this two-week simulation game,
a ninth grade teacher with special competence in economics was
invited by two teachers of top track eighth grade social studies
to plan and run the whole operation. The dilemma of the game
was the negotiation of a new three-year contract for laborers in
a factory manufacturing "Widgets."

The *situation* was that the current contract, a three-year package, soon to expire, called for a 75ᶜ per hour increase over the
three-year period—25ᶜ per year for each category of worker. The
students were given information appropriate to the roles they played.

Each union worker had an individual blank financial balance
sheet extending over three months. The group's decision was based
on an analysis of individual financial records.

As one would imagine, the involvement was intense and the
maneuvering adept, for these were sons and daughters of owners,

managers, professional personnel as well as a few semi-skilled workers. They asked teachers about, and, though officially ruled out of order, did "buy" spy information from opposing camps as the negotiations reached a fever pitch. It goes without saying that insights were deepened regarding the "Unresolved Problems in Income Distribution."

For our purposes, several comments should be made. (1) This was a creative, functional augmentation of the prepackaged curriculum, adding elements to the learning environment that really turned the trick originally intended by the authors of this experimental unit. (2) The teachers applied valid economic principles as operational constraints in the development and execution of this simulation. (3) Comprehensive, appropriate, realistic economic information was supplied to each group. (4) A staff member was assigned as a continuing advisor (umpire) of operating groups to see that rules were followed and that necessary time limits were set and followed. (5) The cooperative staff group made necessary adjustments in the available information, rules, and deadlines as the game progressed. (6) An extensive evaluation of success or failure of each performing group was fed back to students through post-game, discussion critiques. (7) In a sense, this was an "extra official" curriculum change in that it modified a program outside the official curriculum planning group which had worked two years on the preparation of this new unit.

It is my assumption that instructional leaders must allow sufficient latitude for this kind of "extra official" curriculum change if they really expect creative teachers to make learning environments responsive to the different and changing needs of boys and girls.

Initiating and supporting approved one-year and two-year textbook studies with a view toward adoption

Now for a moment let us turn to more mundane, highly structured efforts to bring about curriculum change. Every teacher, every department, every school and school district faces the need for efficient procedures to decide about the selection of new instructional materials, especially textbooks, for which the annual outlay may represent 2% of the total expenditure of a district. It should be noted that in today's situation any real intent to individualize instruction and to make the best use of a variety of old and new materials makes almost impossible any attempt to hold rigidly to a single set of official procedures for the selection and adoption of materials.

However, there still remain some basic deadlines, basic personnel involvements and relationships, basic financial constraints, and basic investigative procedures which cannot be ignored except at the hazard of appalling waste in staff man-hours and incriminating piles of poorly used or unused books, instructional kits, and AV materials.

Consequently, our basic pattern is something like this:

August-November: Elementary principals and secondary departmental chairmen are solicited for the identification of textbook studies they wish to make. I have a simple form, "Requests for permission to study textbooks for adoption," to solicit this information.

December-February: Official textbook study committees and chairmen are designated; the criteria for selection are formulated in each study; assistance is given in securing appropriate examination copies for the committees; and committees narrow the selection down to two or three.

March and April: After intensive examination of the two or three leading texts, each committee formulates its recommendation in one of the following ways:

1. recommends revised edition of current text,
2. recommends adoption of a new single textbook to be distributed to all students in a particular grade and subject,
3. recommends adoption of a single textbook, as above, plus classroom sets of one or more texts,
5. recommends pilot use of one, two, or three leading textbooks, thus extending the process into a two- or three-year study, or
6. recommends continuation with present text and the local production of supplementary materials during the summer or the next school year plus the following summer.

April and May: Recommendations of the committees are reviewed and approved by the Administrative Council and the Board of Education.

May and June: Orders for new textbooks are placed by individual schools and, in Missouri, paid for out of any remaining
textbook funds (from State) before the end of the fiscal year,
June 30.

These thoughts occur to me as I review our efforts to streamline
materials selection procedures to fit the changing conditions. It would
appear that simple and carefully designed in-class testing of new
materials by pilot teachers will become the general nature of our
revised process for evaluating and selecting new materials. The
formalization of a school or district-wide decision will come only
after the fact of a very convincing local classroom demonstration
of the appropriateness and effectiveness of tested materials. This
will make the investigative end of the process very open, both
to the multitude of different materials and to the great variety of
student population and classroom situations throughout our district.

Regardless of our revised procedures, it would seem a minimum
requirement that at the end of each study the recommending group
should be able to come up with substantial, professional reasons
(a copy to be filed in the curriculum office) for the decision it
has made. And that report should be accompanied by the revised
course outline by which the new textbook was selected.

Let me mention one final thought about textbook studies. We
should not be led to believe that pilot use of materials is a simple
or sure answer. Our seventh and eighth grade mathematics teachers
studied and piloted materials for three years before making a final
decision, only to apply in the next summer for an IPC-sponsored
project to develop locally a supplementary workbook of some one
hundred pages.

Designing, developing, and implementing revised
or new courses over a period of one or two years

At this point I should like to consider an Arena Three curriculum
event that involved the principals and selected teachers from three
secondary buildings during a recent span of two years. It has to
do with the solidification and refinement of our journalism program,
grades seven through twelve. This project serves as a good example

of the mutually supportive roles which must be played by *teachers, instructional coordinators,* and *principals* for the proper development and implementation of new learning environments for students. As mentioned before, these three kinds of staff members seem to make up the ideal instructional leadership team in the public schools.

The high school journalism teacher launched the project with this memo to me and the secondary principals:

> To: Dr. Frank—, Mr. Richard—, Mr. George—, Mr. Edward—
> From: Barbara—
>
> Enclosed please find a copy of the proposed journalism program for grades seven through twelve which John—, Joyce—, Joyce—, Joan—and I have been considering and planning since late November. We are excited about the potential of this program and feel it could be an effective one.
>
> We would like to meet with you at some early date to explain our feelings about this outline and to hear your reactions to it . . . etc.

The principals and I met with the journalism teachers, agreed with their proposal, and suggested that they apply for some released time to plan the implementation of the program the following fall.

Subsequently, the group applied for one day of released time to work in the Instructional Planning Center. A thirteen-page report resulted from that day of released time. The activities of the seventh grade journalism club were outlined, with dates assigned. An eighth grade sequence was projected on the basis of each week being divided into two segments: a three-day instructional sequence and a two-day independent work unit during a regularly scheduled class period. A detailed production schedule was projected for the regular ninth grade journalism class, with eight issues planned for the next school year.

In the same manner, the group outlined the after-school sophomore journalism program, the sequence of study of the eleventh grade Journalism I, and the production schedule of Journalism II. A letter from me to the State Supervisor consummated the official establishment of the ninth grade course as a unit in practical arts.

In February of that year the journalism teachers again requested and received some released time to revise plans for the next school year in light of their year's experience. The net result is an exemplary seventh through twelfth grade journalism program for our students.

Researching, designing, developing, and implementing comprehensive curriculum change in a subject area over many grades and many schools

Social studies is probably the most highly prized and jealously guarded content area of the public school teacher. A curriculum dealing mostly with traditions is most difficult to move out of a traditional approach. In this regard, it is probably second only to worship services in our churches and synagogues.

A school does not really develop and implement a "new" social studies curriculum. At best, it spawns a new generation with only a few characteristics clearly distinguishable from the parent program. Nevertheless, I believe that the ten-year effort in our district to revise the social studies will serve as an interesting illustration of the intense thought and management maneuvering that is required to realize some visible face lifting of such a benign curricular countenance.

A little history seems necessary to set the context for the "beginning" of this particular effort. During my first fall with the district (over a decade ago), the Board of Education and teachers' association joined forces in offering a five-lecture series on the basic principles of economics. The immediate impact of the series was disappointing, but it did cause deep thought about the problem of economic education in our schools.

Over the next two years, three steering committees of selected staff from our schools and professors from Washington University, Principia College, and Southern Illinois University formulated and had approved district-wide goals for economic education, political science education, and geographic education.

One point of view made clear by each of these statements of goals was that "achievements and characteristics [of any social system] are properly studied in the context of [their] societal values, customs and traditions, physical environment, and discoveries and technology. The superiority of these achievements and characteristics is in terms of and relative to these contextual factors.''

In terms of our first quality check, namely, the examination of the objectives of a curriculum change, this above comment clearly signaled in the early years of our effort that our revised social studies philosophy would assume that there are many (pluralistic) ways to meet man's diverse needs, and one's own way is only one.

During these same two years, a team of six elementary teachers compiled a guide, *Instruction in Personal Finance and Economics K-12*, which provided a conceptual framework for teaching personal finance and economics plus brief descriptions of ninety-eight successful "experiences" and "studies" in personal economics conducted by elementary teachers in our district the preceding year. Also during that same period, resource guides were written by secondary teachers, giving junior and senior high social studies teachers ideas about how to treat the economic aspects of civics, ancient and world history, and American history.

At that point in time, several of us became concerned about the many disjointed efforts and materials taking the time and energies of our staff without any over-all end product in view. Cooperative curriculum work done with Dr. Harold Berlak in the new Social Studies Center at Washington University and long conversations with key members of our staff prompted me to propose a more systematic, comprehensive attack on the whole complex problem of revising our total K-12 curriculum in social studies. The combined secondary and elementary administrative councils granted us permission to re-focus our effort and revamp the groups needed to launch the new attack.

You might find it worthwhile to apply our first and second quality checks to our total social studies project by noting the disciplined deliberations and scholarly research which went into (1) the identification of revised objectives, (2) the formulation of a new conceptual framework, and (3) the selection of content and approaches to aid the student in his acquisition of basic social studies concepts and skills.

In the fall of 1966 a district-wide Social Studies Steering Committee K-12 was formed. It met a full morning once a week for the first semester of that school year, and almost as frequently the second semester.

The first task of this group was to draft a statement of philosophy, or rationale, for the teaching of social studies in the Ladue School District. At a general staff workshop in April, the committee presented its proposed "Rationale for Social Studies K-12." There were three parts in the rationale. Part I stated our belief that the role of the social studies disciplines was (1) to provide a definitive and consistent language for describing social phenomena, and (2) to provide some theoretical principles for predicting the outcomes of social interactions of a given kind, in a given place and time.

Part II contained a diagram representing the committee's empirical view of how man functions in a pluralistic society to meet his needs and wants in a constantly changing physical and technological environment. The diagram used in that workshop is reproduced in Figure 4-1.

Part III contained a theory of human learning which made explicit the committee's assumptions about (1) the nature of the learner, (2) the important elements in a learning environment, (3) the process of interaction between the learner and the environment, and the products of this interaction.

The staff's general reaction to that presentation was: "Okay, that's great theory. Now, tell us what it all means in terms of what and how I teach social studies in my classroom." To answer that request, several elementary principals and dozens of teachers worked three summers in the Ladue Instructional Planning Center producing *eleven* complete, original social studies units for grades 2 through 6, plus the adaptation of another about Mexico.

During those three years we produced the following units:

Grade	Theme	Titles of New Units
2	Man Meeting His Social Needs	1. *3R's: Roles, Rights, Responsibilities*
		2. *How Groups Function* (A colony on Venus)
		3. *Sudbury, 1638* (A Puritan village)

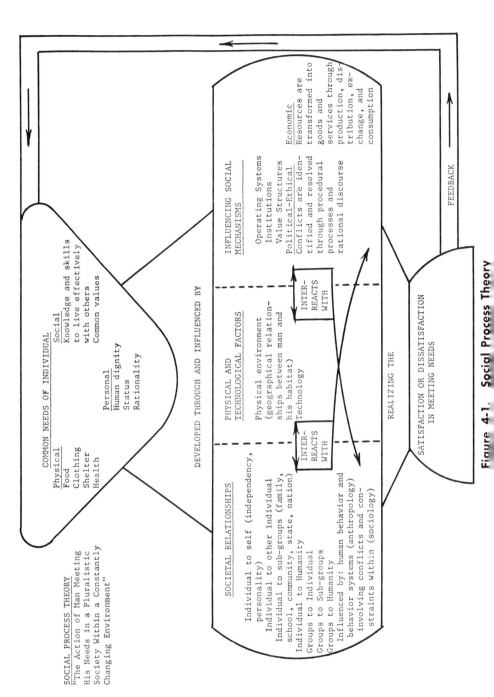

Figure 4-1. Social Process Theory

114

Grade	Theme	Titles of New Units
3	Man Meeting Physical-Social Needs in Ways Influenced by Physical and Technological Environment	4. *Meeting Group Needs* (Hershey town) 5. *Mexico* 6. *Tarabamba* (A Peruvian hacienda)
4	Man Meeting Personal Needs in Ways Influenced by the Institutions and Values of His Society	7. *Finding the Way to Dignity, Status, and Rationality* (Famous people) 8. *Meeting Personal Needs in a Group Setting* (From classroom to Amish)
5	Changes in Ways of Meeting Needs Analyzed in Light of Influencing Factors of Sociological Relationships, Physical and Technological Environments, Institutions and Values (Rural and Semi-Rural America)	9. *Cultures in Conflict* (Contemporary Navajo Indians) 10. *Riverside, U.S.A.* (A small town experiencing some of the benefits and problems of urbanization)
6	Changes in Ways of Meeting Needs Analyzed in Light of Influencing Factors Same as Above (Urban Centers of the World)	11. *Urbanism: A Way of Life* (Including a brief study of pollution problems) 12. *Social Order* (From King John's England to present-day St. Louis)

Figure 4-2 is a reprint of the last page of an article in *Educational Leadership*, May 1970. By flow chart and commentary it gives an overview of our working arrangement for the revision of both elementary and secondary social studies up to 1971.

In terms of our "third quality check," mention should be made of our special efforts for "communicating" the new units to teachers. Teachers who authored the units were the leaders in

Figure 4-2. Flow Chart re: Social Studies

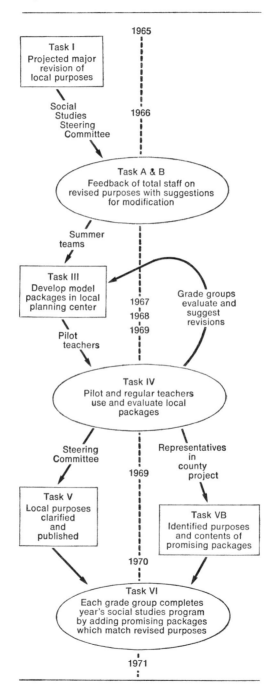

1965

Task I
Projected major
revision of
local purposes

Social
Studies
Steering
Committee

1966

Task A & B
Feedback of total staff on
revised purposes with suggestions
for modification

Summer
teams

Task III
Develop model
packages in local
planning center

1967
1968
1969

Grade groups
evaluate and
suggest
revisions

Pilot
teachers

Task IV
Pilot and regular teachers
use and evaluate local
packages

Steering
Committee

1969

Representatives
in
county
project

Task V
Local purposes
clarified
and
published

Task VB
Identified purposes
and contents of
promising packages

1970

Task VI
Each grade group completes
year's social studies program
by adding promising packages
which match revised purposes

116

1971

this phase. First, they piloted the units with students; second, they directed the IPC in making minor revisions; and third, by demonstration, video-tape, discussion, and conferring, they assisted all other teachers on each given grade level to prepare themselves to teach the new units to their students. Feedback from the total group of teachers was then used to determine what, if any, major revisions should be made in the new units during subsequent summers.

For our fourth kind of quality check we might ask: What feedback existed to signal successful achievement of curriculum change in terms of the learner's behavior? As in the case of the great majority of efforts to change curriculum, this is the weakest link in the whole process. We find ourselves dependent upon teachers' observations, parents' remarks, and our own observation of student response as our subjective data for determining the success of changes. These are totally inadequate from a scientific standpoint.

We are in the process of strengthening the arm of our research-evaluation department. The "action research" design of two decades ago was built around the "spilling out" of these kinds of data as a natural consequence of any planned change. We need to recapture some of that spirit and technique.

In summary then, let me list the several quality-control features which were evident in our persistent effort to revise the K-12 social studies program. The revision was preceded by more or less intensive study of the disciplines of economics, political science, and geography. A system-wide but small steering committee then assisted the Coordinator of Instruction in grinding out a rationale to guide us and the rest of the staff toward the design, production, and implementation of new methods and materials. The supportive production services of an instructional planning center were crucial. A well-thought-out system of instructional planning enabled broader involvement and more efficient production by staff. Well-selected consultants used in carefully planned in-service sessions provided a sound informational base for early deliberations. Pilot testing and evaluative reporting of the strengths and weaknesses of the new units served as effective means for disseminating methods and materials to the larger staff. Periodic confrontations with total staff were used to keep them informed of the progress of the steering committee, task force, and production teams.

And the final question: What forces and paraphernalia existed to maintain this curriculum change? Each elementary teacher has two or three complete resource units which are concrete models of the objectives, methods, and materials intended by those responsible for its design. In addition, each elementary principal and teacher, along with each secondary social studies teacher, now has a 51-page *Teacher's Handbook for Social Studies K-12*, produced by the Ladue Instructional Planning Center. Here are some excerpts from the Foreword:

> This handbook is provided to give each teacher the overall goals, underlying structure, and current listing of offerings in our K-12 social studies program.
>
> The handbook also attempts to say what seems to be expected of the teacher for the effective implementation of these offerings.
>
> In the appendices will be found articles which have relevance to the content, methods, and design of our revised social studies curriculum.
>
> We feel that this handbook signals the transfer of the collective effort of many people into the responsible hands of all teachers of social studies in the Ladue School District. It is hoped that what is recorded here will help in that transfer.
>
> Coordinator of Instruction K-12

Describing the many-faceted three-and-a-half-year project "Innovation 68" at a suburban high school

A Kettering Foundation sponsorship precipitated a radical departure in curriculum and instruction in our high school. Four hundred 10th-12th graders out of 1500 enrolled in academic courses on a weekly schedule of one lecture, two small group seminars, and two independent study periods. A team of eighteen teachers worked six weeks during the summer of 1967 repackaging the entire academic curriculum in Unipacs. Revisions and expansions followed the next two years.

It was the on-site visit of a representative of the Kettering Foundation that launched us into this significant project of curriculum renewal. The occasion of her conference with the superintendent, the high school administrators, and me remains sharply imprinted on my mind. When asked for her comment, she said: "Where are the innovations?" There was a dead silence; so quiet that I thought I could hear the blood pressure rising in the circle of administrators. We had a good school, but it was a traditional factory for the production of graduates seeking admission in the best colleges of our nation.

The exchange that followed ultimately uncovered the plan of one of the assistant principals for meeting the individual needs and special interests of our 1500 senior high students. Let me define the *purpose* of this project by quoting from a pamphlet published by the Director of Dissemination for "Innovation 68."

Two goals emphasized during the planning stages continue to influence the direction of the program today:
(1) the program should make provision for students' individual learning rates and learning styles, and
(2) the program should place more responsibility on the student for organizing both his time and his learning procedures as a preparation for college.

When the assistant principal was appointed Director of Innovation 68 in the spring of 1967, he listed the *following principles* which were to guide staff in the *development, implementation,* and *evaluation* of the new program:

1. The student should begin his instruction at his present level of achievement. (Student evaluation through testing and teacher observation will be necessary to determine his level of instruction.)
2. A student must be allowed to proceed in each subject area at his own rate. (This will vary from student to student and for each student from subject to subject.)
3. A student must grow in ability to make individual decisions regarding the use of 40% to 50% of his time while at school.

4. Each student should receive guidance from a counselor and each subject matter teacher in setting his immediate and long-range goals.
5. The student's post-high school plans should be a guideline in determining areas of study and emphasis placed on each area.
6. The student should confer with teachers and his counselor regarding organizational and planning techniques for reaching goals.
7. Teaching procedures and instructional materials should contain a maximum of automatic feedback to the student concerning his individual progress in his academic studies.
8. Teachers should be alert to evaluate, in addition to subject matter progress, the student's change in ability to make decisions as well as attitudinal changes such as increased curiosity, critical thinking, and his attitudes toward independent intellectual growth.
9. The laboratory and seminar approach shall constitute a major portion of the learning procedure.

I have placed in Appendix B† a part of a Unipac so that you might have a concrete idea of the curriculum that the student faces in "Innovation 68."

The weekly format for "innovation" courses provides special opportunities for what our staff believes to be *improved communication* regarding the topics under study. First, large group lectures that go with each packet are thoroughly prepared and effectively presented by the team member (three to four teachers on each subject area team) most interested and competent in the main topic of each packet. The small seminars encourage research, presentation, and discussion by the students more under their own direction than their teacher's, except, of course, the prestructured plans contained in the Unipacs and supplementary handouts.

Then, most important of all, in the opinion of both students and teachers, are the opportunities for individual conferences between teacher and student during the independent study time. It is through these contacts that teachers become well informed

---

† See Appendix B.

of exactly what progress each student is or is not making on the assignments. The so-called *feedback* is immediate and specific.

Maintenance of the program seems assured at this point. In just a few years it has grown from the part-time involvement of 400 students to the part-time involvement of all students, since all English classes are now organized under "innovation." Many physical and organizational changes will help to insure the continuation of this program. Space has been divided differently, from large group areas down to individual study and conference areas. The entire curriculum has been packaged as handouts for individual students and resources for students are deployed differently from the traditional patterns. The roles of the students and teachers involved have changed significantly. Teacher aides have been introduced to perform new roles in this revised system. Evaluation instruments and procedures have been changed. Teachers have learned new techniques especially for use in small group seminars. Special in-service sessions trained them in these techniques.

The fact that space, time, grouping, curriculum, roles, materials, teaching methods, and evaluation have all changed as a result of "Innovation 68" serves to point up that ideally all such aspects will change when a staff is successful in making a significant, comprehensive, durable curriculum change.

Developing new diagnostic teaching skills in staff through a comprehensive K-3 research project investigating the relationship of perceptual training and learning styles.

One significant event with which to begin this report of our program to help the disabled learner is a county-wide conference organized and chaired by our Superintendent. The conference represented a culmination point in his personal effort to crystallize a joint attack by the medical and educational professions on the problems of the normal public school student with minimal but specific physical-psychological dysfunctions. Such dysfunctions, though not apparent to the untrained eye, significantly handicap the student in achieving respectable academic progress in the competitive arena of the regular classroom.

This Conference on Learning Disabilities of Young Children

was sponsored by the School Health Committee of the St. Louis County Medical Society in cooperation with the Cooperating School Districts of St. Louis County and the St. Louis County Health Department. Thirty tables of eight participants were each chaired by a practicing doctor, psychologist, social worker, speech and hearing therapist, college professor, or school administrator. The animated buzz sessions of these table groups and the follow-up question and answer periods attested to the superb input of the nationally known panelists: Herbert G. Birch, Newell C. Kephart, James Lawson, and Helmer R. Myklebust.

This event has been cited to illustrate both the energetic leadership of our Superintendent in this cause and the high level of consultation that has been called on to define the approach of this project and to support its implementation. Sound curriculum planning needs both committed administrative leadership and objective, hard-nosed guidance from researchers in fields most related to the problem under study. Dr. Warren Weinberg, Medical School of Washington University is co-chairman of this project.

At one of our project staff planning sessions I expressed what I considered the specific objective of this research project for those of us working on the improvement of instruction. A quotation from my handout distributed at that meeting is included below.

> The instructional personnel understand the objective of this research proposal in the following operational terms:
>
> Given approximately 370 public school children carefully classified as to stages of behavioral, intellectual, perceptual, cognitive, educational, and physical development, we will report the observable effect of describable dosages of a few discrete treatment techniques on the perceptual, cognitive, and educational development of these children over a period of four consecutive school years.
>
> Meeting the objective stated above requires the performance of *two* distinct and very difficult tasks, each of which is a worthy challenge in itself.
>
> I. The first task is to formulate some describable dosages of a few discrete treatment techniques which have some demonstrated relevance to the problem at hand, namely, school children having difficulty in learning.

II. The second task is to administer these describable dosages in an effective, consistent fashion over several classrooms and over a period of approximately four years.

Task number one was accomplished by personnel in our Instructional Planning Center. They selected, adapted, and created instructional plans and materials that served as the "desirable dosages of a few discrete treatment techniques." The four different treatments were named "Visual-Motor," "Auditory-Language," "Multi-Sensory," and "Integrated." The last was applied to the control groups and consisted of a compilation of successful activities used by our teachers the past few years.

For four years these special dosages are being administered one-half hour per day by the regular classroom teacher, the same kind of dosage being applied four years to the same groups of children. Retrospective analysis will be made of end-of-third-grade achievement and the patterns of physical, mental, psychological, and emotional functioning of each child to determine the correlations of achievement with developmental levels and to detect the associated effect, if any, of the experimental perceptual training programs upon these correlations.

One significant point that should be made generally about research-oriented curriculum change is that the wedding of research projects and curriculum development is seldom, if ever, a smoothly functioning marriage. Nevertheless, as in human matrimony, there seems to be no better, more realistic way to attain the ideals that seem inherent in such a joint adventure.

In the education business, we have to immerse research (and the researcher) in the natural rough and tumble of the regular classroom to derive valid indications of what changes contribute toward making a good education. The dilemma obviously is that controlled sampling of an uncontrolled environment leaves you holding nothing more than intriguing probabilities. And these are a rather flimsy reference for designing prescriptive instruction. But what about the immersed, research-practitioner? Is he or she not much better equipped for the next swim? It is my belief that most of the durable innovations in the future will come (as they have in the past) from the researcher-practitioner who tries, assesses, revamps, and reuses changes in his own operational arena.

I would make this brief analysis of our K-3 Project as a module of curriculum change. First, such an action-research project focuses on and is responsive to the actual performance of the learner. The mere fact of this focus makes action-research in terms of my criteria a high-grade curriculum planning project. Second, the commitment to research requires that the practitioner attend to relevant scientific knowledge and to associated inquiry techniques. This most certainly strengthens the reasoned-base for his content decisions and enlarges his repertory of appropriate teaching techniques. Thirdly, action research accommodates and encourages a maximum of face-to-face communication between teacher and student, teacher and instructional leader, instructional leader and researcher, and various combinations of the above. And it is for the most part purposeful, relevant growth-producing communication for all communicants. Fourth, feedback to the various participants is a dynamic and integral part of the face-to-face communication. And finally, its major benefits will endure to the degree that the research-oriented practitioner has further internalized the attitudes, concepts, and skills of the adventurous inquirer and problem-solver.

FIVE

Mediating the forces of curriculum renewal

A catalytic leader is one who facilitates activity between two or more persons or forces without himself being continuously involved.

It takes desire and discipline to be a catalytic leader. You have to have a gut level desire that learners be *more* active in more challenging and responsive environments. And second, you as a teacher, principal, coordinator, or parent have to develop a tactful, yet decisive and disciplined manner for conveying your desire to persons operating in Arena I, II, or III, whatever the case may be. You will then begin to see evidence that by their *own* inventiveness students and teachers will have found more stimulating and productive ways to learn from persons, things, and events in their environment.

An exuberant facilitator of curriculum renewal is to improved learning environments as the right amount of live yeast is to the improved texture of homemade bread. Most *flat spots* in a curriculum renewal project are due to languid leadership at *those* very points in the process.

Leadership in action has been well displayed throughout the previous chapters, particularly in Chapter Four. For example, we saw some instances of the leavening lift that creative teachers could and did inject into their classroom situations (Arena One) to enable students to experience the thought processes, the emotional sensations, and the social interactions intended by the curriculum designers. The impact of an assistant principal's leadership on the overall instructional program in a suburban high school illustrated conclusively the influence that a building administrator exerted in Arena Two. The ten-year program to revise a K-12 social studies curriculum demonstrated several aspects of the crucial role played by a district-wide coordinator in Arena Three.

Yes, curriculum renewal can be harvested in the institutional setting of the public schools, but it takes purposeful, inventive leadership all along the line.

Focusing on leadership

The focus of this chapter is on leadership. It will be on that special type of leadership which we believe stimulates and supports the continuous invention of improved learning environments. As should be expected, what characterizes the leader will characterize the process he leads. In so doing, the means and the ends become one, the usual condition of a social process.

With the focus of this chapter on leadership, it has been organized in the following way. In the first part, we will share with you our best hunches about the personal traits and professional capabilities of effective facilitators of curriculum renewal in our day. These statements will be followed by sections illustrating kinds of action typically exhibited by a coordinator of instruction as he facilitates curriculum change in his situation.

Recognizing the personal traits of a catalyst

The teacher, principal, and instructional coordinator are all basically catalysts who are trying to facilitate in their own operational arenas the interactions of persons with other persons, things, and events. It is the common belief of such practitioners that a balanced, varied diet of such transactions causes each person to have a better understanding and acceptance of himself as well as a more valid, functional picture of his total environment; most importantly, other people. The psychological aspects of these transactions have been well hypothesized in the book, *I'm OK, You're OK* by Thomas A. Harris.

It appears to me that there are four elements to be found in good measure in the perceptions of the inventive instructional leader.

First, it is my hypothesis that he has the salutary perceptions of self-acceptance and self-insight like those of the adaptive-type, self-actualizing personalities hypothesized by Maslow and others. These perceptions provide the instructional leader with the internal fortitude and purpose necessary to survive, with some relish, the constant buffeting of the stormy interactive experiences that make up the daily dict of the change agent. To the degree that he possesses these affective reservoirs and cognitive insights, he is blessed with more maturity and integrity than the majority of his fellows.

Second, it is my hunch that you would find the instructional innovator slightly more sensitive to signals of potential in human beings and more positively oriented to auspicious occasions for upgrading the human condition. Such perceptions give him a greater built-in readiness to act and a greater kit of usable options.

Third, I would strongly hypothesize that the instructional facilitator has open, positive preconceptions of other people in general which allow him to relate deftly and comfortably with persons of varying talents, tendencies, and temperaments. Such perceptions permit him to engage and disengage with equal alacrity as the needs for such varying relationships come and go.

Finally, I would suggest that the instructional catalyst possesses a broad and deep perspective of the unifying ideas and universal processes that make man and his environment appear as one whole, continuous, dynamic phenomenon. To the degree that he has such a grand view of life, he enjoys a more commanding vision than the majority of his colleagues.

The modest inference, then, is that the ideal and most successful catalytic leader combines the personal integrity of the psychotherapist, the sensitivity of the superior teacher, the people-oriented and task-oriented creativity of the best administrator, and the unifying perspective of the philosopher.

Though they cannot be separated that cleanly, let us turn from personal traits and look at the professional capabilities needed by an educational facilitator.

**Signaling the essential coping capacities of
an educational catalyst**

Rather than identifying an endless list of particular professional capacities that are needed at one time or another by the educational change agent, I have chosen to identify some persistent tasks that such a person faces and to comment generally about the concepts, skills, and attitudes involved in the effective coping with these tasks. In some instances, particular performances have been described either to give concrete examples of what is meant or to report a technique that has proved successful in the experience of this writer.

At this moment I can think of seven persistent tasks which the educational catalyst must handle competently. These are:

(1) affirming a rationale for the change process as it relates to learning, teaching, and supervising,

(2) analyzing the difficulty of a group and offering specific assistance,

(3) interlocking inside and outside supporting services,

(4) facilitating communications inside and outside all operational arenas,

(5) managing a flow of little and big decision-making,

(6) keeping one step ahead of critical pressures from inside and outside, and

(7) seeking involvement inside and outside the district for personal and professional renewal of the facilitator.

Each of these tasks will be considered in varying degrees in the remainder of this chapter.

**Affirming a rationale for the change process
as it relates to learning, teaching, and supervising**

If a catalytic leader is to have leverage, he must set goals and procedural guidelines for himself which are sufficiently dissonant with the objectives and practices of enough other people in his operating arena to cause them to seriously reassess the adequacy of their own conceptualizations and skills. *Our power to bring about change begins with our own desire to reach goals not yet achieved, be we catalytic agents, teachers, administrators, parents, or students.*

How does one evaluate the services of a change agent? *The accountability of a facilitator of curriculum renewal must be judged ultimately in terms of the theoretical base he uses for justifying the alternative materials and methods he selects for improving learning environments.*

Any parent, student, teacher, principal, coordinator, or central office administrator who wishes to effect a rational, systematic renewal of the curriculum in his arena *must take a stand regarding some rationale for the change process* as it relates to learning, teaching, and supervising.

I found the following rationale (curriculum theory) helpful to my colleagues and me as we worked to improve learning environments for our students.

Proposition I. Learning is a power system of individual growth toward new dispositions and capacities through interaction with existing animate and inanimate systems in the learning environment. Or stated another way, *the power of learning is in the response of the learner to the environment.*

Proposition II. Teaching is a power system for facilitating the interaction of individual growth systems with existing animate and inanimate systems having established goals (dispositions) and resources (capacities). *The power of teaching is in the sensitivity of the teacher to the response of the learner to his environment.*

Proposition III. Supervision (or coordination) is a power system for sensitizing teachers (1) to the nature of individual growth systems, and (2) to the probable influence that existing animate and inanimate systems will have on individual growth systems when they interact. In other words, *the power of instructional supervision is in deepening and sharpening the sensitivity of the teacher to the response of the learner to the environment.* An effective strategy for upgrading this circular process is to intervene at the point of instructional planning.

Proposition IV. Curriculum planning is a power system for disrupting and recasting the established patterns of interaction between existing environmental systems and particular individual growth systems, for the purpose of eliciting specific individual growth toward preselected dispositions and capacities. This then takes us back to Proposition I and completes the cycle of learning to teaching to supervising to curriculum planning, back to learning.

Propositions V through XI are more extensive analyses of the phenomenon of curriculum planning as defined in Proposition IV.

Proposition V. If one wishes to bring about an effective disruption and a valid recasting (i.e., curriculum planning) such that there will be substantial change from former patterns of interaction, he must directly involve as many as possible of the current operators of existing instructional systems in the re-examination and re-definition of the same. For the assumption is that the changes these operators bring about in their own attitudes and skills through this involvement are the influential factors that will create and incorporate new functions and forms into the revised program called the ''new'' curriculum.

Proposition VI. A close re-examination of instructional systems and their established patterns of interaction will reveal that such instructional systems are subsystems of larger physical, economic, political, socio-cultural systems of the local community, state, nation, and world.

Proposition VII. Operators in the larger outside systems such as youngsters, parents, community leaders, and scholars should be involved in giving feedback and ''feedforward'' to the curriculum change process, to insure that instructional programs are appropriate subsystems of larger social systems in the eyes of these consumers and patrons of the public school.

Proposition VIII. Division of labor (lay and professional), through phasing and sharing of tasks, should be used in the over-all process of curriculum planning in order to capitalize on the expertise of different groups and to provide the checks and balances of varying points of view. Crucial in this cooperative process are mechanisms and procedures by which early functioning groups arrange for preliminary involvement of the next group, if the second group is to be a true flowering of the first.

Proposition IX. The organization for curriculum change should be developed according to the principle of *form* follows *function*. The administrative "line" organization of the school system should function both corporately and individually as policemen designating which curriculum matters are to receive the attention and in what order. The composition and procedures of all so-called curriculum bodies should have an ad hoc status, designed specifically to fit the nature of the task designated by the administrative group.

Proposition X. Content and method are equally important in curriculum change, just as they are in teaching and learning.

Proposition XI. Instructional specialists working with teachers and administrators are necessary to coordinate the people, events, and things that must be effectively involved in the constant renewal of instructional plans. Such specialists should have a "staff" relationship to all school personnel, including easy access to all levels of the permanent "line" organization. The special perspective of such system-wide instructional specialist should be such as to assure appropriate articulation of all programs from grade to grade and prudent balance among the various curriculums of a comprehensive educational experience.

Reference back to the organizational charts in the early part of Chapter Two should be helpful in clarifying much of what is stated in the above propositions regarding curriculum planning in a school district.

The remaining sections of this chapter will contain descriptions and guidelines for the working style of a district-wide change agent. However, it is the belief of this writer that most of the generalizations that will be drawn about the working style of an Arena Three change agent can be applied equally to change agents operating in Arenas One and Two. In other words, it should be assumed that the teacher, principal, and coordinator face similar curriculum planning demands and need similar leadership skills. As said on page 18 of this book, the facilitator of curriculum renewal in all instances is one who can stimulate and nurture increased inventiveness in persons working in learning environments.

Analyzing the difficulty of a group and offering specific assistance

It is quite often the case that the change agent must sense the difficulty faced by a group in its effort to move through the change process. Having sensed it, he must bring to the attention of the group a useful resource (such as a procedure, a publication, or a person), or he must directly launch the appropriate procedure, create and distribute the needed document, or assume the role of the resource person needed at that moment.

I am reminded of a not-too-distant rash of drug abuse situations in our district, and the several meetings that our administrators were having to make decisions about how to implement a preventative program of drug abuse education. On one occasion this coordinator sat silently through an entire meeting of our administrators with representatives of the juvenile court. It dawned on this coordinator after that meeting that one difficulty was the apparent confusion over their separate responsibilities as related to the use of authority in the control of student behavior.

A synopsis of my post-conference remarks on that occasion is given in the next few paragraphs to illustrate how a change agent can play the role of observer to clarify the problem faced by a group.

I pointed out that the jurisdiction of the school arose from its administrative authority over the schools, whereas the jurisdiction of the courts arose from the authority exercised by the law enforcement agencies of the state. Hence, logically and legally, there could be no jurisdictional disputes between law enforcement agencies and the schools. However, considerable friction could be generated when the two bodies did not see eye to eye regarding the best way to handle the same aberrant behavior having educational, administrative, civic, and criminal aspects.

Further on I commented that when civic and criminal laws were broken by adults or youngsters in the school or on the school campus, the school officials should call in law enforcement agencies or bear the risks of legal suit by either the law breakers or the victims of law breakers for the way in which the school officials adjudicated and assessed penalties for each case. Then I added that another reason for the close cooperation with law enforcement agencies in cases of illegal acts was to reduce the possibility of double incrimination for a single offense. The separate, uncoordinated meting out of penalties by the school and the courts might quickly compound the suffering of the offender far beyond what was intended by either agency and become so devastating as to remove all possibility of future rehabilitation through the efforts of either agency.

One closing observation in that document might be of interest to school people and parents. It was merely the statement that school rules frequently reflect and relate to constraints of dress, language, grooming, and manners arising from customs and mores rather than from civil and criminal laws. In such cases school officials find it impossible to formulate rules in any specific relationship to the plurality of customs and mores of the larger society. Such rules, when established, have to be justified on the basis of minimizing factors in the learning environment that would interfere with the achieving of educational goals publicized by the school.

The generalization to be drawn from the above illustration is that the change agent must do many things to maintain within himself the ability to either secure or become the variety of resources which groups will need as they are engaged in the curriculum change process. The difficulties are legion, so the need for help is increasing.

One way for the change agent to strengthen himself as a direct resource to problem-solving groups is to be a voracious consumer of popular and professional non-fiction literature, without restriction to field or topic. Frequently, a concept or analogy of some totally unrelated field can be applied in an effective, oblique fashion to give a refreshingly new slant to some underfoot irritation. One must read reviews in popular periodicals as well as professional journals to locate leads to promising pieces. *The Saturday Review, The Christian Science Monitor*, a couple of weekly news magazines, one metropolitan daily, a weekly national educational news service (*Education U.S.A.*), plus at least one professional journal at each level of the educational hierarchy would seem to be a minimal index to current reviews. The contents of our local professional library are described in Chapter Six.

Interlocking inside and outside supporting services

The change agent must make the most of continuous stimulation and confirmation from persons concerned with education, curriculum planning, and the improvement of instruction. Of first importance to his effectiveness as a local operator are his contacts with persons of the local staff and local community as described in Chapter Three. Of next importance would be his more or less continuous, though less frequent, contacts with regional and state groups, be they voluntary lay and professional associations, private enterprises, or governmental bodies having some official relationship to the school district, such as community educational television, teacher training institutions, or the state department of education. And finally, at least two strong national contacts can be justified, one to the voluntary professional association of the coordinator's choice and the other to the appropriate subdivision of the U. S. Office of Education such as the Instruction, Organization, and Services Branch or Cooperative Research Branch. It would not be unusual for the general instructional coordinator, during any given year, to exercise ties with a half dozen national, professional associations.

Contacts with persons in the groups cited above are of many kinds under differing circumstances. Nevertheless, it is not difficult to make the judgment that the most valuable kind are the individual, personal acquaintanceships which develop over years because of common interests and compatible personalities. The circumstances of one's actual involvement run the gamut from attending conferences, to consultation to or from the agency, to ultimate extensive cooperative work on some joint project. Certainly, active participation and office holding in one's local, state, and national professional associations should never be underestimated as sources of stimulation and support for the frustrated novice or the battle-scarred old-timer.

**Facilitating communications inside
and outside all operational arenas**

The work station of the effective teacher, principal, coordinator, or administrator often takes on the appearance of a message center more than anything else. There is usually a steady flow of messages into the practitioner's arena. In a similar fashion, information about the needs and activities of each operational group must be properly directed outward to agencies who can meet its needs or who have to approve its activities.

Another whole set of communications are those created within each operational arena having to do with the planning, procedures, and progress of that group, be it a teacher's class, a principal's staff, or a coordinator's instructional division.

As one illustration of what I mean, let me summarize the kinds of communications handled by a district-wide coordinator as described in his log of one day's actual operation.

Letters, memoranda, and oral information received: One letter from a state association president and another from an assistant state commissioner of education concerning a professional conference being planned jointly by those persons . . . A notification from the district's materials center that sample Amherst Project Units had been received as requested . . . A half-hour demonstration of a new Japanese 16-mm film projector . . . A fifty-minute observation of a ninth grade economics class . . . A luncheon conversation on school finance with junior high teachers . . . An appointment with a high school physics teacher who was applying for an overseas teacher exchange assignment . . . An elementary principal's request for some professional books including *Crisis in the Classroom* . . . Another principal's written recommendation about a speaker his teachers felt they would like to hear during in-service . . . The scanning and filing of numerous circulars on commercial educational products . . . An appointment with the high school chairman of practical arts about the issues to be raised in a coming departmental meeting . . . A meeting with two junior high typing teachers and a junior high principal to hear their proposal regarding typing standards for ninth graders . . . A purchase order to be approved for two hundred copies of a federal source book on drug abuse for staff in-service . . . A preview copy of a 36-page booklet about the district's visual arts curriculum to be distributed to fifty art educators visiting the next week.

Letters, memoranda, and oral information sent: A written memorandum to elementary principals to accompany a 25-page elementary science report instructing them how to analyze the report before attending the coming principals' meeting . . . A note to a ninth grade social studies teacher accompanying sample instructional materials on economics and consumer education . . . Oral instructions to a film projector salesman regarding how he should proceed to bring his new machine to the attention of all principals . . . Oral request to an elementary principal to investigate possible schedules and costs for using a consultant as recommended by his staff . . . Oral recommendations to junior high typing teachers about formulating new standards by which to grade ninth grade typing students . . . Written memorandum to an elementary principal accompanying a set of filmstrips and records he had consented to preview.

The generalization to be drawn from the above listing of communications in and out of one school station is that purposeful, timely, continuous two-way communication is a crucial function of all facilitators of curriculum renewal.

Managing a flow of little and big decision-making

The above vignette of the catalytic leader in action is not complete without some special word about his individual decision-making process as he determines what to do or not to do at a given time and place. Sitting at his desk or touring the field, the instructional coordinator must have some mental screens and managerial adroitness which help him quickly sort out:

(1) what should be coded and filed figuratively and literally (a most important file in each case being the discard file),

(2) what should be perused and then filed,

(3) what should be selectively circulated (e.g. possible purchases or announced conferences) before further action and final filing,

(4) what should be assigned for processing by others and then filed,

(5) what should precipitate *related* action by the coordinator or an associate and then filed (such as an application to attend a workshop or scheduling visitations or conferences in pursuit of an aroused curiosity),

(6) what should be placed on "hold" while research and pre-

liminary planning prepares the way for taking some appropriate direct action,

(7) what should be placed in a deferred "come up" file on a date pertinent to its deadline (a speech or written report), its predicted ripening (seasonal), or its anticipated timeliness in terms of related contingencies (budgeting for materials if new courses are approved),

(8) what should be responded to immediately in writing, by phone, or by conference (including notes of thanks and congratulations), then filed with action recorded,

(9) what should be initialed, with or without comment, and passed on per indicated route or returned to sender,

(10) what should be filed in the folder of the appropriate coordinating body to come up on its next agenda, the chairman of the group being notified if it is someone other than yourself,

(11) what should be noted on your pocket, desk, or wall calendar and then filed, and

(12) what should be kept visible under a desk top paperweight until you can resolve what appears to be an appropriate disposition from (1) to (11) above.

Keeping one step ahead of critical pressures from inside and outside

Of first importance to the catalytic leader is the anticipation of scheduled and to-be-scheduled events. As has been implied earlier in this book, *there are seasons and cycles for curriculum change*. Let me reiterate that fact at this point because many of the decisions described in the previous section have to do with proper timing of the appropriate action on the part of the change agent in terms of an amazingly large number of seasons and cycles in the development and operation of a school district's programs.

Obviously, of fundamental importance are the several *annual* calendars operating in the life of the district. There are at least a half dozen that I think of immediately: (1) the school year for students and parents, (2) the school year for teachers, (3) the school year for certificated administrators, (4) the employment year for non-certificated personnel, (5) the fiscal year from July 1 to June 30, and (6) the calendar year from January 1 to December 31 with all its customary patterns for Americans.

Associated closely with these above annual calendars are several in-school operational cycles. Those that come to mind immediately are (1) the cycle of admission and placement of students, which are generally keyed to birth dates before and after October 1 at the elementary level and basically related to credit accummulation and course selection at the secondary level, (2) the cycles for the development and official addition or dropping of units of instruction at the elementary level and course offerings in the secondary schools, (3) the cycle of guidance services to students and parents regarding curriculum offerings, (4) the cycle for selecting and requisitioning new equipment and materials, (5) the Board of Education cycle with annual election of members and reorganization, (6) the cycle of levy and bond issue elections, (7) the cycle of county, state, and federal distribution of funds, (8) the cycle of hiring certificated and non-certificated staff, (9) the yearly set of local and state professional conferences, and, in addition, an endless variety of annual activities described in this book that deal with aspects of staff in-service and the refinement of instructional plans and materials, such as course revision and textbook changes. (See Appendix C, Processing Cycles for Curriculum Development in Ladue.)

Then add to these calendars those cycles that are more than one year, such as curriculum cycles described in the latter part of Chapter Six. Included in such cycles are (1) curriculum developments involving many grades or many subjects and sometimes extending as long as five years; (2) pilot studies with a year for planning, a year for implementation, and a year for evaluation; (3) repeated annual workshops to parallel three to five years of curriculum development; (4) one-and-a-half to two years' budget planning to encompass the interaction of operational and fiscal budgets; (5) extended bond issue revenue cycles over several years; and many others that the coordinator is reminded of when he faces decisions relating to them.

Many of the above current calendars may be kept visible to a coordinator on his hook and loop 3' by 5' wall calendar. Others are recorded throughout his desk and pocket appointment book. Even with this much vigilance, occasional events will be overlooked and schedule conflicts will arise which temporarily disrupt or retard the flow of intended progress.

Of equal importance with the change agent's anticipation of scheduled and to-be-scheduled events is his sensing of trends and new goals in the whole business of public education. Information of such trends comes from both lay and professional sources. Wherever it comes from, the change agent's knowledge of such current thinking crucially influences his decision-making as he nudges the course of internal events in one direction rather than another. The story of in-service told in Chapter One reveals a nudge back in 1964 which is still exerting considerable effect on the current curriculum efforts in our district.

All of this suggests that the curriculum coordinator must have innumerable personal contacts and active lines of communication with all sorts of lay and professional thinkers if he is to have a valid, up-to-date sense of trends and new goals in education. With this kind of perspective he can determine the significance of very small beginnings that are symptomatic of desirable or undesirable conditions and trends. He can then know what to do, or not to do, for preventing the wrong developments and for fostering the right. This kind of perception and vigilance permits him to use current analysis of operations as "feedforward" guidelines regarding next steps and/or the incorporation of new constraints. Richard Evans of Salt Lake City sometime ago delivered one of his powerful two minute messages addressed to the importance of paying more attention to early signs and small beginnings in all aspects of life if one wishes to make the most of the present and the future.

Earlier in this chapter, as well as in Chapter Three, this coordinator has described the organizational structures and operational functions that give him periodic, if not continuous, personal contacts with students, parents, teachers, and administrators. Added to this should be the constant to occasional contacts he enjoys with the non-certificated staff. Such contacts often provide him with a unique blend of the lay and professional point of view, plus bits of information known only to them because of their special position from which to view youngsters and staff. Also, let us not overlook the highly useful personal and professional contacts outside his district, through which the change agent is exposed to an entirely different perspective of his school system.

During such personal contacts the change agent must have his "sensors" out for signs of student boredom or excitement, teacher indifference or enthusiasm, parent resistance or support, administrator apathy or initiative, and scholar criticism or praise. He must correctly interpret acts of student alienation, teacher rebellion, and principal veto. He must assess the genuineness of new parental and administrative expectations. He must prudently evaluate the seriousness of a student request or complaint, or a teacher's compliment or objection, of a parent's "scapegoat" song or real disillusionment, and of the administrator's challenge or arbitrary demands. He must maintain close contacts with local, state, and national colleagues who can corroborate the commonness or uniqueness of the stresses, strains, and prods felt in his own situation.

All of these contacts ideally must be open, two-way channels of authentic information. The structure for providing such internal contacts comes almost automatically to a central office coordinator. All he needs to do is use his opportunities and elaborate on them. Outside the district it becomes his responsibility to build a network of lay and professional contacts through participation in community organizations and professional associations. These are the kinds of roots by which the change agent has access to the nutrients necessary for the development and maintenance of effective educational services.

The balanced growth and full flowering of an instructional program result ultimately from the flow of the information acted upon by the energy and values of all persons functioning in the local school district.

And finally, there is reading. This source is a great contributor to the coordinator's ability to keep one step ahead of critical pressures. And in our McLuhan age, add to reading all multi-media sources of information. These indirect contacts with other persons' thinking have inestimable impact on the change agent's thoughts and commitments. All of us are annually the observers of hundreds of hours of television.

It would be a serious dereliction of duty if a curriculum change agent were not an active reader of both established and current pieces in professional and popular literature. He must be the developer and greatest user of the district's professional library. Ladue's is described in Chapter Six. As part of the library service there must be a broad flow of professional periodicals. At home, the coordinator must have a supplementary stream of popular periodicals and books.

At school, at home, and in the car, electronic forms of mass media must add to the steady shower of data impinging upon the change agent and his associates. Add to this the professional and popular films, filmstrips, and slides as well-tailored and exciting packages of relevant information.

Given the coordinator's attention to multiple, related calendars, to personal contacts with a great variety of lay and professional people, and to indirect contacts (mass media) with the larger, past and present community of thought, he should be successful in keeping one step ahead of critical pressures from inside and out.

Seeking involvement inside and outside the district for personal and professional renewal of the facilitator

The coordinator's involvement extends from one-to-one conversations with students in the classroom to long distance telephone calls to authors of current educational best sellers. The order in which many types of involvement will be listed does not imply any hierarchy of value. Rather, the value to the coordinator appears to depend on how many or how few of these involvements he is able to keep an active part of his day-by-day and year-by-year modus operandi.

At the time of this writing, this coordinator is involved in a set of sixty to seventy classroom visitations, which will give him direct contact with students and teachers participating in Ladue's new social studies program. To listen, to observe, and to occasionally teach some of those classes was deemed to be the only way for the coordinator to collect millions of specific unadulterated impressions about the impact and problems of that program. His general impressions after having completed that two- or three-week tour should be at least one valid body of knowledge to use in the further development of that program and other programs similar in structure. The greatest value of such visits to the coordinator should be that he becomes better equipped to visualize proposed programs in terms of the predicted response of youngsters.

Conferences with teachers following visitations like those above provide this coordinator with the opportunity to support teachers in their genuine effort to make valuable learning experiences out of the plans and products made by someone else. An equally discernible value of such follow-up conferences is the chance for the coordinator to learn the teacher's honest feelings and evaluation regarding the new programs. Such reactions are among the most pragmatic criticisms of a new curriculum. Many of the adaptations that earlier teachers have found necessary to help students achieve the lesson's objectives are incorporated in later editions for the use of other students and teachers. One instance like this was reported in Chapter Four, involving a sixth grade unit on "Social Order."

The involvement with summer production teams has proved to be a most auspicious way to work with teachers in depth on the design of learning environments, including the production of some of the materials and activities to be used. It is then that the local staff has sufficient reason and time to develop systematically the overall rationale of a unit of instruction, behavioral objectives, teaching strategies, resource materials, and criterion tests that do in fact increase the probability of the expected student performance being elicited. Under these circumstances the instructional specialist reaps tremendous benefits from the creative outpourings of the experienced, imaginative, dedicated teacher.

Presenting and discussing the new programs at parent-teacher gatherings invites the parent's unique critique of the whole process of curriculum change. Through such involvements the coordinator is reminded to what extent the professional team has or has not fulfilled the parent's expectations for the schools. The normal reaction is a split decision, usually with many more for the change than against. However, such shallow, infrequent involvements of parents often precipitates sharp criticism from those holding extreme views, especially if the subject is social studies. The coordinator, being a practitioner and not a theoretician or researcher, must learn to steer a curriculum course that runs somewhere down the middle of the range of political, economic, social, and ethical views of the people in his district. After all, they are the group paying the biggest part of his salary and the parents of the youngsters with whom he works.

Occasionally, the coordinator will work with a lay committee on a curriculum project over an extended period. Such an approach should increase the likelihood that the particular expectations of the local community will be served and a middle course more precisely established in the case of controversial issues and topics. We have had lay committees working in the areas of economics, sex education, and drug abuse. The reason for these particular committees should be obvious in light of previous comments.

The coordinator becomes involved with personnel from food and custodial services when he is engaged in the business of setting up workshops and conferences. As already mentioned, listening with a special ear at those times will net some differently biased views of staff, students, and programs.

This coordinator has found it necessary to organize, promote, and evaluate some regular schedule of interschool grade level and departmental sessions. *Such interaction and communication does not occur naturally.* And any school system's effectiveness diminishes with the lack of such exchange of ideas and support. The running of such a monthly enterprise gives the coordinator an opportunity to work with several key principals and department chairmen in the planning and successful execution of such in-service sessions. This development of leadership and dispersion of responsibility for curriculum change is a sine qua non for any change agent who expects to affect many subject areas at many grade levels in many schools. Ideally, you have in this group of leaders a loyal force that effectively spreads and maintains your influence throughout the school system.

Working with the elementary or secondary principals on a weekly basis should have a similar effect on the establishment of a system-wide set of over-all instructional goals. These persons are in charge of what can be called control and support systems, without which the instructional systems could not function. They must keep you apprised of potential problems with control of students, staff, materials, and equipment that might cause the downfall of an otherwise good instructional program. Imagine the havoc that is wrought when the closed circuit system breaks down in our TV world history course involving several classes. In a like manner, principals must alert you to overload of personnel or technological support systems that might cause a breakdown, one of the most common being the *overburdening of the teacher* with impossible combinations of management and instructional tasks. Students, too, can be overstressed, as was the case the first two years of our new modular program in grades 7, 8, and 9. We had junior high youngsters rushing through the most complicated, the most demanding, and the longest school day of any group in the district.

Our nine coordinators have found it beneficial to meet regularly once a month even though all of our official work is accomplished in small joint efforts within our group or with other members of the school staff. The need is one of communication, review of common goals, and exchange of useful operational techniques.

The best condition for involvement with the superintendent, his assistant, and the business manager, beyond the regular principals' meetings cited above, seems to be a more or less constant state of accessibility. We are on call for ad hoc conferences and enjoy rather rapid accommodation of our requests for brief appointments.

Upon the recommendations of staff and the approval of the superintendent, the instructional specialist secures local, state, and national consultants for working with staff groups, including the coordinators themselves. The services of the local coordinator have been greatly strengthened by the judicious use of good consultants. This has occurred at all points along the curriculum change process, namely, in the identification of needs, the analysis of those needs, the planning and production to satisfy those needs, the implementation of the improved programs, and the evaluation of their impact.

Extensive illustrations of the varied use of consultants may be found in Chapter One and elsewhere. It could be estimated that on the average our district uses ten to fifteen consultants each year for our efforts in curriculum development and instructional improvement. Some of this activity will be treated again in Chapter Six under the budgeting for curriculum renewal.

The occasional teaching of evening and summer college courses on methods and curriculum is a valuable professional experience for the instructional coordinator. Leadership in local, regional, and state workshops also helps keep the instructional specialist up-to-date in his professional reading, as well as more crisply aware of what he is in fact trying to accomplish in his daily operations.

Usually there are some speaking engagements, papers, articles, and pamphlets that force the coordinator to organize his reflections about his activities and his plans for the future. Frequently, such assignments stem from his participation in local, state, and national professional associations. To have to address remarks to a variety of lay and professional audiences is a valuable developmental experience.

SIX

Creating a "friendly" environment for curriculum renewal

Just as the previous chapter was focused on leadership style, this chapter will be focused on "friendly" conditions under which such a leadership style will flourish. What are the prerequisite conditions that support the work of curriculum change agents, be they students, teachers, parents, or administrators?

One overriding condition is the general climate for change. All facilitators of change early in life acquire a keen sensitivity to the prevailing attitude toward change. They then tailor their efforts according to what seems feasible in terms of these prevailing attitudes. Consequently, the over-all climate of a school-community situation has an amazing effect on what can and does occur by way of curriculum renewal.

As pointed out earlier, the top lay and professional officials of a school district are the main determiners of the climate for change. It is through their personalities and deliberations that such climates are established, maintained, and modified. Their assigned role is to shape policies for the local schools based upon their loyal and insightful translation of the insistent local social-political pressures amidst the influences of the larger world.

It can be reasonably assumed that there is a mixture of "friendly" and "hostile" attitudes toward change in most school districts. History has usually shown (e.g. sex education) it takes a healthy majority of "friendly" attitudes toward change for innovative efforts to become established, improved learning environments. For if such is not the case, the countering forces will so discount the good and exaggerate the bad effects of each and every change that disaffection will rise, divided commitment will falter, and reactionary forces will ultimately win the day.

I shall attempt to illustrate these contrasting attitudes as they are exhibited by persons holding different points of view. I realize that such an attempt may elicit images of false dichotomies and educational myths that I will not have time to dispel even if I could. Nevertheless, the point to be made is so significant to effective curriculum planning that it must be made even in the face of these hazards.

I have a hunch that people who contribute to a "friendly" environment for curriculum renewal are those who assume that *all persons* in a school situation are *potential* facilitators of the learning of any and every person in a given classroom, school, or district-wide arena. All persons perceive each other in a helper-helpee relationship. All have equal readiness to ask for or to give help depending upon circumstances. Obviously, I have stated this as an ideal. Such an ideal will be seen by many as an extreme "process" point of view, or some other equally devastating appellation.

On the other hand, I have a hunch that persons who contribute to a "hostile" environment for curriculum renewal are those who assume that selected adults are guardians of a narrow set of prescribed social-intellectual skills, a stringently required repertory of provincial heritage, and an exclusive hierarchy of social-ethical precepts against which the learning and development of any and every person is to be judged in a given classroom, school, or district-wide arena. All persons perceive each other as competitors in a struggle to achieve those selected skills, concepts, and values which will enhance their survival and accelerate their rise in the social structure of their classroom, school, and district. Those learners disadvantaged by deviant physical and intellectual characteristics, social-emotional deprivations, or different cultural backgrounds are destined to be considered a drag on the effectiveness of the school, be they students, teachers, parents, or administrators. I know that the above overdrawn picture will prompt some to attach the label of the "content" point of view. In any event, the extremes have been designated.

These extremes are probably just the school's version of the larger society's struggle over the competing values of stability and change. Perhaps all one can expect is that school curriculums at least keep up with the changes that have already occurred in that larger society. Only by doing this can the school discharge its assigned role of releasing each learner's power to become a fully functioning member of that society.

It is intended that the remainder of this chapter will point up some varied personnel and material resources, flexible operational procedures, and functional inter-personal relationships which are needed in an environment "friendly" to curriculum renewal. One criterion test to confirm that you have achieved a "friendly" environment would be to collect and evaluate evidence that there was *increased power* on the part of students, teachers, parents, and administrators to bring about changes in the curriculum. For if this has occurred, the curriculum specialist has "husbanded" the means for releasing student and staff efforts in the never-ending process of curriculum planning.

Identifying school district subgroups and services that are essential for the support of curriculum renewal

The official organizational groups of a school district are the board of education with an appointed professional executive officer, a school building staff under the leadership of a principal, and a class of students under the control of a teacher. These groups with their respective leaders constitute a line of authority well suited to the implementation of well-defined, established educational and administrative services. And all is well as long as the system deals with similar populations in a secure and static environment.

However, in our society, populations shift and the environment is constantly being transformed. Given a few radical changes in such factors as the background of students, parent expectations, financial resources, occupational opportunities, and mass communications or other technology, the school system finds itself needing more *the ability to change its services* than the ability to maintain them.

Consequently, without a doubt, the first order of business for a would-be change agent is either to find or to create *subgroups able to define and to facilitate the changes in services* which the system should make, such subgroups being somewhat different from the official administrative bodies directly charged with maintaining on-going operations. In other words, the change agent has to assume a major responsibility for creating organizational substructures which are "friendly" toward curriculum renewal.

One of the basic characteristics of such subgroups should be that membership consists of representation from many levels and from different horizontal divisions of each level. Such vertical and horizontal representation from the total organization will equip the subgroup for direct and immediate reading of where operations are obsolete, eroded, or misdirected. Also, subgroups of this composition will have the vision and talents to formulate some well-founded hypotheses of how the operations ought to be changed.

Another basic characteristic of such subgroups is that their membership consists of individuals who can act as liaison to the official bodies holding the authority and mechanisms for implementing modified services once such have been developed.

One such subgroup in a school district might be a parent-teacher district council composed of the key school administrators and the officers of the several parent-teacher associations. Another might be a special task force committee with membership from parents, administrators, coordinators, teachers, and students. Still others would be instructional councils made up of administrative and instructional staff from many levels and students from different grades, or instructional steering committees of students and teachers, with one or two administrators serving as liaison to the official structure. A high school might have a *student* curriculum committee with a few departmental heads as staff representatives.

The would-be change agent has a second order of business that follows close on the heels of *organizing change-facilitating subgroups*. This second order of business is the *courting of existing service groups* plus the *creation of new service groups* who are needed for special support to the development, production, implementation, and evaluation of curriculum changes, that is, improved learning environments. Existing service groups who need to be courted are custodians, secretaries, nurses, librarians, counselors, maintenance crews, and business office personnel. Service groups which might need to be created are teacher aides, audio-visual assistants, special teachers for individualized learning centers, psychometricians, instructional coordinators, and a special team for operating a district center for the planning and production of instructional materials.

Obviously, such added human resources would make a district much more "friendly" toward and capable of offering continuous revision of its learning environments. However, the change agent has to see that these services remain services and that they not become empires that feed upon rather than serve the district.

As further guidance to the would-be curriculum change agent, the following generalization might be observed about the characteristics of "friendly" subgroups and service persons. The value of such groups and persons appears to reside in the degree to which they serve one or more of four functions. (See the Curriculum Renewal Cycle in Chapter Three.) Together these four functions make a school system more adaptive, that is, more able to make soundly tailored, appropriate changes: (1) such groups more accurately and quickly identify the new purposes to be served, (2) they provide the special expertise and resources for developing usable plans for achieving the identified purposes, (3) they facilitate the effective implementation of new goods and services, and (4) they furnish feedback regarding the impact of the revised services.

Probably this last function is the least-well-established in most schools. Many of us have just begun to set up comprehensive feedback systems which will give us a more or less continuous collection of evaluative data on the cognitive, affective, and psycho-motor progress of our youngsters. Once our feedback is more multi-dimensional and precise, it should exert increased influence on those subgroups identifying new directions for curriculum planning. From a systems standpoint we would then have created a much stronger curriculum renewal loop for our school district.

Because a great variety of administrative subgroups and service groups are the prime social mechanisms for carrying out the above four functions of curriculum renewal, examples of such groups and what they do will be discussed in the remaining sections of this chapter. The sections will deal first with the organization and operation of change-facilitating subgroups, then the courting of existing service groups, and finally the creation of new service groups.

The purposeful functioning of these groups will insure a proper measure of knowledge and skill for optimum curriculum renewal. Then, when given the aforementioned positive attitude toward change, the environment is totally "friendly" for curriculum improvement.

Organizing administrative subgroups to identify new purposes

A change agent new to a situation, or newly inspired to do something, is immediately in need of involving himself with subgroups, formal and informal, who can help clarify what needs to be revised. If you have been appointed to a position of instructional leadership, it can be assumed that the power structure which has given you the mantle of catalytic leader has also committed to you sufficient financial and administrative support, at least for a honeymoon period. However, for a long-term marriage you will need to establish functional subgroup relationships to help you survive as a challenger of the status quo.

Do not be misled into thinking that the initial assignments handed to you by the hiring administrators correctly identify what is most needed in the situation. On the other hand, prompt response to what they think is needed is a very necessary performance to strengthen your relationship with them. And in the final analysis, they are the comptrollers of the power and latitude you exercise as a catalytic agent.

Capitalizing on staff interest from the beginning

As implied above, probably the first move of a change agent faced with an immediate list of assignments is to identify and organize ad hoc administrative subgroups who can investigate the problems and make some initial recommendations regarding purposes, approaches, ingredients, and evaluations of the suggested new services.

This coordinator is reminded of the first-day request made of him to develop a reading improvement service for secondary students. By the second week, he had arranged a special luncheon meeting with an administrative subgroup including a junior high principal, the school psychologist, and an experienced elementary teacher who had been selected to launch the secondary reading improvement program.

After several planning sessions and visitations to area schools and private agencies working with poor readers, we drafted some over-all recommendations about how to proceed, plus some specifications of materials and equipment. These were ultimately presented to and approved by the board of education so that some services were inaugurated by mid-fall of that first year. By the beginning of the second year we had laboratories established and staffed by a full-time specialist in each of our secondary schools.

Our recommendations to the board had contained the promise of periodic follow-up reports on the impact of the program on participating students. The instructional coordinator relied heavily upon the services of the school psychologist for collecting and reporting this feedback. At the end of three years, that research team compared the changes in reading efficiency index (rate times per cent comprehension) of the participating eleventh graders with that of nonparticipants as per three subgroups: the lower third in class rank, the middle third, and the upper third. Since the participating and nonparticipating groups were nearly equal in size, since comparisons were made between groups having similar class rank, and since the post-testing was done a year or more following the special six weeks of training, the demonstrated superior gains of the participating students convinced the board and the study team of the positive effect of the reading improvement program.

The point to be emphasized about that project is that the subgroup of principal, psychologist, teacher, and coordinator had sufficient expertise and liaison to administrative and instructional systems to plan, implement, and evaluate a new learning environment in three secondary schools. Today, on a short- or long-term basis befitting student needs and/or interest, individual assistance in achieving improved reading skills is still available to all of the secondary students of that district.

Developing administrative subgroups for coordinating several areas of instruction at the same time

Another early move for a change agent faced with a long list of assigned projects is to identify staff members who can be catalytic leaders in one or more areas. The ultimate result of such a process in a school district of five thousand or more will be the establishment of part-time or full-time coordinators for each of the eleven or twelve curriculum areas of a comprehensive public school program.

It was the school psychologist, functioning as the director of special services, who was most ready and able in our district to assist the curriculum office in a long-range effort to improve the elementary reading program, as well as in the secondary program mentioned earlier. We formed the Elementary Reading Steering Committee, which functioned only for the duration of the three-year study. On the committee were the school psychologist, two elementary principals, a basic skills teacher, plus part-time involvement of thirty selected regular teachers and all remedial teachers throughout the district.

In three years this subgroup had led the staff in the production of a reading guide containing: Section I, "Criteria for Grading and Evaluating Student's Ability in Reading"; Section II, "Minimum Standards of Phonic Elements and Skills Introduced at Various Grade Levels"; Section III, "Phonics for Ladue"; and Section IV, "Core Reading and Writing Vocabulary, Grades 1-3." A year later, another basic skills teacher and her principal developed, piloted, and distributed a "Word Analysis Test" to screen an individual student or an entire class at the fourth grade or above.

Pairing sets of elementary principals and their staffs, the curriculum office organized similar administrative-instructional subgroups which worked on language arts, spelling, science, and social studies. An interesting historical note is that K-6 guides for reading, language arts, and science were completed by the end of the second year while social studies, a much more difficult task, was completed nine years later.

The guideline being illustrated here is that through the shared leadership of the principals, coordinators, and key teachers, all members of an elementary staff can experience in-service training (mainly the clarification of present program) and involvement in the production of curriculum guides. This type of visible, organized in-service is a traditional auxiliary supporting service for curriculum coordination. Its main value is that it helps staff clarify what it is attempting to do in each subject area. There is good sharing of ideas, but little, if any, significant change in learning environments. An *invisible,* fully integrated type in-service (discussed elsewhere) seems more productive in the long run.

At least four conditions seem essential for the success of visible, organized in-service: first, the staff members must be working on matters which closely relate to their performance in the classroom; second, a minimal regular calendar of accommodations must be established and officially supported; third, continuing leadership must be assigned to each group; and fourth, resources must be equally accessible to all groups.

I still like my statement on coordination made to the Administrative Council during my first week on the job:

> *The heart of coordination*
> Coordination of instruction is realized through the cooperation of all persons charged with the responsibility for the teaching in our schools. Simply stated, these persons are of three types, (1) the administrator of a school building or system, (2) the instructional specialist, including all teachers and supervisors or directors of special subjects, and (3) the coordinator of instruction.
>
> Whatever the program change being contemplated or being introduced, each of the above three types of persons should be involved and informed. When any two members of this triumvirate are working on a curricular change, they should keep in mind the interest of the third party and should inform or in some other way involve him in action being contemplated or taken. This in many instances will call for duplicate memos being distributed to all parties concerned.

The Director of Music and the Director of Physical Education had well-developed and well-coordinated programs before I arrived on the scene. They were encouraged to continue what they were doing as well as to consider additions or deletions to their programs as changing circumstances seemed to require. One such case for the Director of Music was the development of a string program beginning at the fourth grade. This was accomplished with the aid of some additional staff and the active support of principals. Now for the first time, we are developing sufficient string players to form orchestras in all of our secondary schools.

In the case of the Director of Physical Education, the first curriculum planning project was the redevelopment of the health program for grades seven through twelve. The director, the high school health teacher, and this coordinator created a guide which is still the basic framework for the district's health instruction today at those grade levels, although methods and materials have changed in response to changes in student interests and social issues.

Using administrative subgroups to establish criteria for the selection and use of readings for secondary English classes

The cooperative roles of principals, teachers, and coordinators were very well demonstrated in a recent junior high project. The need arose to develop guidelines for the selection of readings to be dealt with by individual students or groups of students in our revised language arts program, grades 7 through 9. A student, a couple of parents, and some staff members had raised some objections to words found in one piece selected by a summer task force. An investigation was authorized by the Administrative Council for the purpose of creating a rationale, criteria, and procedures to guarantee a more relevant and acceptable selection of literature by students, teachers, and parents in the future.

In the words of the Coordinator of Language Arts, "I was very much in the background on this project. It was the principals with their English staffs who wrestled with this complex problem of selecting materials most useful in terms of the interests and maturity of our students and at the same time most effective in terms of the goals of our language arts program. Since they produced the guidelines, there is great likelihood that they will be followed.

Besides, it was an important professional experience for each participant." And I would add: "So was the experience of the Administrative Council, as it reviewed and approved what the staff group had produced."

This operation was a good illustration of what I mean by *invisible in-service*. It was known only to those involved, hence invisible. It was conducted as an integral part of the staff members' work in each of the two buildings involved. Using their on-going classes as a resource, staff members had immediate opportunities to test and apply skills and concepts being developed, thus assuring greater validity and greater likelihood of future application. Finally, all persons to be affected were involved, leaving no immediate problem of dissemination or implementation.

A guideline to be reiterated at this point is that the involvement of principals is essential to effective curriculum change. It was our assistant high school principal who developed and implemented the comprehensive organizational change, "Innovation 68", described in the latter part of Chapter Four. Acting in a similar fashion a few years earlier, a junior high principal had made a research proposal regarding interdisciplinary teams. This was in part an outgrowth of the district Task Force Report described in Chapter Three. This proposal included the addition of a specially designed new wing to that junior high and ultimately the organization of the entire seventh grade program in that building according to the basic guidelines of the original proposal. Staff involvement was intensive and extensive over several years, all carefully designed.

For the next few sections, permit me to share with you the thoughts I have about how many common in-service activities and regular service groups can be cultivated to give more friendly support to curriculum renewal.

Making in-service training more supportive of curriculum renewal, with or without consultants

Both visible and invisible in-service are needed to support curriculum renewal. My emerging conviction is that the invisible, very businesslike in-service session of the small operational group is the more effective. Such sessions are an integral part of the on-going work schedules. In our district we continue to encourage new ways to accommodate this kind of in-service.

Appropriate in-service training must be seen as an essential component of all aspects of curriculm planning and instructional improvement. Sessions such as those on "Realities of Learning", related in Chapter One, must be staged when the staff is seeking new perspectives of its purposes and tasks. Long, frequent in-service deliberations like those of the Social Studies Steering Committee described in the middle of Chapter Four must be launched and maintained when a new over-all design is being created for a large K-12 segment of the total curriculum. In-service production teams must be spawned, counseled, and sustained through periods of initial frustration, first-draft labor pains, and final publication pressures such as those of the visual arts department portrayed in the middle of Chapter Three.

Once a production team has completed a published guide and has recommended materials for the implementation of a revised program, the coordinator needs to establish training sessions to facilitate teachers' comprehension of new concepts and their acquisition of new teaching techniques for the most effective use of the recommended materials. Such was the case of our modern K-6 mathematics program, developed in the sixties. Three elementary principals, two secondary mathematics teachers, and three mathematics-educational university consultants formed the core production team for that project. To assist teachers in the gradual implementation of this program, one consultant, Dr. Larry Miller of Ripon College, conducted district-sponsored mathematics workshops during four subsequent summers, the last one held recently to refresh old staff and to orient the new. Similar-type sessions have been conducted in our district this year for those schools which have moved toward an adoption of the SCIS and SAPA elementary science curriculums.

Special workshops were conducted for members of the high school staff who were working with the "Innovation" classes described in the latter part of Chapter Three. That was another case of sessions used to help staff acquire concepts and skills crucial in the implementation of the new program. Under the auspices of the Kettering Foundation, training was provided in the writing of "unipacs," small packets designed to give individual guidance to students about the objectives, activities, resources, and expected student outcomes in each two- or three-week unit of the course. In other sessions, under such consultants as Dr. Jim Smith (Abington, Pa.), "innovation" teachers were involved in the analysis and practice of small group teaching techniques. In Chapter Seven there is a report of recent work with the English teachers which focused on the cultivation of more productive interaction in small group seminars. They wanted to learn techniques to cause effective changes in students and improved human relations within the small group, as well as intellectual gains.

Appropriately organized in-service meetings can also be used to accomplish the assessment of a program's impact and the diagnosis of what still needs to be done. This was well illustrated by the questionnaire-survey meetings organized and conducted not too long ago under the direction of our Coordinator of Language Arts. Part I of the survey asked teachers to report what method, materials, and time they used for teaching aspects of reading, listening, speaking, literature, written language, spelling, handwriting, dictionary, library, grammar, and creative writing. These surveys were distributed to teachers during a staff meeting, completed in a few days, and returned to the Coordinator.

Part II of the survey asked the teachers for their opinion of student performance in five categories: reading, listening and speaking, written language, literature, and other areas of language study. Because the Language Arts Task Force was hoping to get each teacher's personal judgment regarding the performance of students coming to him, Part II of the survey was conducted simultaneously in several joint staff meetings dispersed throughout the district and under the personal direction of members of the Task Force.

Following a brief introduction at each gathering, the four-page survey form was distributed to the assembled teachers. Task Force members whispered clarifications to those who had questions about how to interpret an individual item. The silence was broken only after all had completed and handed in the survey. Those who wished to were invited to remain for a discussion of their response to the whole instrument. That proved to be a valuable interchange (and others like it which followed on subsequent days in the individual buildings), for it increased the teachers' readiness for later discussions concerning which student performances were rated lowest by the greatest number of staff and which areas, therefore, would need investigation and revision if teacher expectations were to be met.

A half-day workshop was then planned in which elementary grade groups attempted to digest the identification of deficiencies and strengths of student language performance as reported by their own group. Under the leadership of the committee, they asked: Do we accept these results? If not, what action would we take? What do we now do to help students deal with these tasks? What district-wide effort do we recommend? It is hoped that such deliberations will lead teachers to a revised perspective of the language arts goals in our district. Report of the final outcome will have to be made in the future.

As in most operations, it is the careful identification of the purpose of an in-service session that guides the coordinator and his planning group to the proper organization and operation of a successful workshop. Several legitimate purposes of in-service are well illustrated above. However, it can be said without hesitation that in the complicated process of curriculum planning, there will continue to emerge new combinations of program improvement and staff growth that will call for slightly different types of in-service. In each case the planning group must divine the function to be performed before it designs the form that will be right. Chapter Seven contains some guesses about future purposes and the shape of tomorrow's in-service programs.

Cooperating with other departments of research and evaluation, guidance, pupil personnel, special services, librarians, nurses, and volunteer parents

The involvement of various special departments in effective curriculum planning has already been well documented in Chapters One through Five. Some reiteration of their role at this juncture should provide additional acknowledgement of each department's contribution to the whole process.

Only with the help of the research specialist can the curriculum planner become more analytical about what factors do or don't contribute to students' achievement of desirable performances. With such increased analytical power he can more assuredly identify practices that will have a predictable good effect. The constructing of effective instructional activities involves the thoughtful application of proven practices which aid the learner in accomplishing a desired performance. The elaborate K-3 Project described in the final section of Chapter Two is a good example of our attempt to use the expertise of a research specialist to improve curriculum planning—in that particular case, to aid the primary youngster with learning problems.

The four-year development of our eighth grade social studies course, American Issues, was interlaced with testing instruments and questionnaires designed in part or in whole by staff members under the leadership of our Coordinator of Research. Assurances from these test results that our students were achieving historical concepts along with skill to analyze issues prompted us to disseminate the revised curriculum throughout all eighth grade classrooms by the end of the fourth year of that project.

As mentioned earlier, we need to do more of this type of evaluation in our district. It is the only way we can objectively show the relationship of curriculum changes to changed student performance. It is important to note that commercial standardized tests are being designed to provide more specific information about the strengths and weaknesses of the performance of individual students. Items more discriminating of different levels of cognitive skills are being included, and the number of each type is being increased to improve the reliability of the user's diagnostic interpretations. Such instruments in the joint hands of the research and curriculum specialists should make educational accountability a much more attainable goal.

Counselors must see that all students have optimum accessibility to all parts of the instructional program. Also, guidance services and the department of pupil personnel must keep the instructional staff apprised of recent knowledge of the common characteristics of different age groups, their developmental growth patterns, and the dynamics of their behavior. Basic to all curriculum decisions is our knowledge of the nature of the learner we arc trying to help achieve some valued concept, skill, or attitude. For example, such factors as the one-year-earlier physical maturation of today's youngsters is obviously a most important consideration for the designers of a sex education curriculum. It was a first grade teacher on our Language Arts Task Force who said, "We must review recent research on language development in children before we revise our language arts instruction."

Guidance personnel must keep us schooled about the importance of the self-concept in the learning process and how self-concept is affected by the conditions for learning arranged by the instructor, especially his own personal relationship to the learner. The concepts and skills like those contained in Glasser's *Reality Therapy* or *Schools Without Failure* must be incorporated in the over-all philosophy of revised curriculums and in the individual learning situations of the instructional units. How we classify, group, and grade students probably has more enduring influence on the emotional, social, and intellectual development of youngsters than all of the clever learning packages devised either by the local teacher or the industrial-educational complex. After all, the dynamics for growth lie within the learner, and if these are short-circuited, all the challenge and encouragement in the world will do no more than produce a partially functioning personality.

For the mass operation which the public school is, it takes a special services division to diagnose the learning problems of the atypical, nonachieving student and to offer therapeutic instructional conditions and materials to help him learn in spite of his disability, be it emotional, neurological, conceptual, or social. The matching of instructional technique with the child's learning style is an educational practice just beginning to be made available through high calibre departments of special services. And as these professionals identify more precisely the minute steps that make up the laborious progress of the handicapped learner, they expose new features about the basic process of learning for the normal learner. In our district, the Director of Special Services works as an assistant to the Coordinator of Instruction. He has the school physician and the school psychologist on his staff.

With knowledge like the above, a complete array of learning tasks can be deliberately built into the curriculum of the normal child, assuring a balanced, total learning experience regardless of how fast and effortlessly he performs it. New preschool and primary curriculums, structured according to Piaget's hierarchy of intellectual development, are explicit examples of such carefully tailored instructional packages. It is the special service personnel who can be most helpful to curriculum planning efforts when the project arrives at the point of the design and construction of specific learning aids for a particular learning task. The Director of Special Services guided the development of special instructional materials for use in our K-3 Project.

We should print in bold type the significant role in curriculum renewal played by the school librarian. If possible, the librarians should be involved in all curriculum projects. It is a great waste of resource when they are not involved, and it is logistically disastrous if they are not informed early of contemplated changes in instructional programs.

In our situation, the Coordinator of Multi-Media works with the librarians to support them in their effort to offer information to students and staff through audio-visual media as well as print.

When a district can afford certified public health nurses as regular members of its staff at a ratio of one to every six hundred students, these highly trained specialists can function as resource persons for instruction in personal health and safety, growth and development, and community health services, as well as take care of health and accidental emergencies. They are crucial members of curriculum renewal projects in such areas as sex education and drug abuse education.

The contribution of parent volunteers and teachers' aides is hard to measure. Certainly it is true in many situations that the availability of learning centers, clerical services to teachers, and supervision of social and recreational activities would all be noticeably reduced without them. Most educators predict a greatly expanded role for para-professionals in the schools of tomorrow.

Cooperating with the departments of staff personnel and school plant

The decisions of the staff personnel department have a more severe and enduring effect on the ultimate implementation of curricular plans than those of any other supporting service. The hiring of native foreign language teachers might critically negate the intended use of an adopted textbook using an Americanized audio-lingual approach. The complete turnover of a department in a given secondary school can send its program off on a tangent completely divorced from any interschool departmental planning of previous years. The lack of released time for departmental chairmen or other key personnel can greatly retard the progress of pilot programs and the development of revised or new course offerings. Seventy-five per cent or more of the character of the instructional program is directly attributable to the background, education, and personality of the teacher, which will change very slightly over a career.

Staff selection can reinforce directly the provincial point of view of an instructional program, or liberate it through a deliberate hiring of teachers with diverse backgrounds and training. The curriculum specialist will find it difficult to predict what the ultimate form will be of a course in anthropology taught by a Bible-belt Baptist, or a course in population geography taught by a Midwest isolationist. As has been said before, the teacher always makes his peculiar translation of any prior curriculum planning.

The recommendation, therefore, is that the staff personnel department and the curriculum department continuously discuss their purposes and their current strategies for achieving those purposes. In those discussions it should become clear where disruptive contradictions exist and what adjustments should be made by either party to bring purposes more in line and to apply strategies mutually beneficial to those compromised, common goals.

Some limited involvement of the instructional coordinators in the staff selection process can help in the correlation of these functions. However, administrators must exercise the prime responsibility for hiring personnel, since they are the evaluators of teachers and the ultimate adjudicators of whether a teacher is promoted, retained, or released, based on his total effectiveness on the job. It should be added that once a new staff member is hired, it becomes the combined responsibility of administrators, coordinators, and teachers to orient the newcomer to the goals, programs, routines, and paraphernalia of his new position.

At least one word must be said about the construction and maintenance of the school plant. Here is where the imaginative,

professional insight of the school administrator becomes most opera-
tive. Of course, the best laid plans of schoolmen are often voted
down by the citizens. So, a supporting PR system can be crucial
to all operations. Without any attempt to document it, let me state
that the lack of the appropriate space or the poor maintenance of
equipment and facilities greatly handicaps the operation of an effective school program. We are just now trying to secure an addition
to our high school, and we find it is no easy job to convince the
citizens of the significant relationship between appropriate space
and better education. My guess would be that if your total community
relations (PR) program has been selling an instructional program
throughout the years, you will have little trouble buying buildings
and equipment when you need them.

Paying the bills for curriculum renewal

School costs throughout this country have risen at a faster
rate than the total economy. The public generally has become very
critical of these costs and has called educators to account. Education
is basically no different from other human enterprises. If it is to
advance economically, it must realize an increase in the amount
of product per unit of human labor. This calls for investment in
technology, in improvement of the skills of the labor force, and
improvement in administrative organization and planning.

School administrators are beginning to adopt planning, prog-
ramming, budgeting system (PPBS) concepts to achieve more effective control over school costs. The over-all goal would seem to
be to reduce those expenditures that do not visibly affect the productivity of the school and to increase those that improve its output.
Educators most expert in management and finance continue to see
promise in the PPBS approach. However, the majority of us are
a long way from understanding how to design and implement such
a system for our schools.

At this moment in our district there is no way to separate
systematically the costs of curriculum planning and instructional
improvement. As pointed out in this book, these processes are

an integral part of all instructional and pupil personnel services. Consequently, it will be only the most visible, clearly definable curriculum improvement costs that will be mentioned here. We must acknowledge that these fall far short of being the total cost for such endeavors.

In the summary which follows you will find a highlighting of some selected categories and accompanying calculation of the percentage of the total operating budget allocated to each.

We have nine central office certificated staff members in the instructional division, whoes salaries represent 01.5% of the total operating budget. We have six noncertificated central office employees whose salaries equal a little over 00.4% of the total. Materials and supplies for IPC printing, IPC AV production, district-wide research, district-wide student testing, and professional library make up 00.75% of the operating budget. Fees to outside consultants for in-service and supplementary salaries to local staff for summer IPC projects amount to 00.22% of the budget.

Calculated on this basis, we have 02.87% of our total operating budget going toward what you might call instructional improvement. I know of no basis upon which to make any evaluative statement about these figures. However, some further comments might be of interest to other practitioners. These are included in the next few paragraphs.

The salary range for the Coordinator of Instruction and his assistant is at the level of assistants to the superintendent. The range for the subject area coordinators is slightly below that of the elementary principals.

The salaries of the noncertificated personnel range from the master printer's pay, which is equivalent to a beginning teacher's salary, through a full range of secretarial rates, down to a part-time COE high school student at a rate under $2 an hour.

An interesting feature of the materials and supplies budget is that it runs far into the red most of the year. The reason for this is that all the supplies for instructional planning projects are initially charged to the IPC account. It is only after the student booklets and audiovisual aids are completed and delivered to the buildings throughout the district that an in-house billing is made to authorize reimbursement to the IPC account from the textbook and audio-visual funds of the receiving buildings. A careful materials cost analysis is made of each instructional item produced in the IPC. Billings to each building are calculated individually on a basis of the number of each item received.

When commercial items are a part of the total instructional package, the IPC instructs each building principal how to formulate his own requisition for an adequate number of each item in terms of his staff and student population. A few frustrating experiences in attempting to centralize the assembling of combination commercial and local packages convinced us that a little paper work was worth a lot of double or triple handling of materials. We also avoided the follow-up headaches on incorrect or damaged shipments. The IPC staff was most happy to have each principal straighten out his own problems with commercial suppliers.

IPC operating funds are used to cover the costs of special requests of *individual* teachers, principals, and central office administrators. Also, there are experimental and pilot projects to be supported which were not anticipated in the budgets of individual schools. Furnishing back-up, emergency funds for unanticipated instructional innovations at the building level is perhaps one of the center's most effective services for encouraging instructional improvement in our district. Most of the audio-visual projects reported in this book were of that kind.

Budgets for in-service are calculated on a basis of $300 a day for top-notch outside consultants down to $50 a day for colleagues from neighboring districts having an expertise we need for a particular task. We average an annual expenditure of about $3,000 for consultants.

By far our major single cost item is for supplementary salaries for staff who work on sponsored IPC projects during the summer or vacations during the school year. We have been averaging about $13,000 each year for such salaries over the past five years.

One final comment on finances. The greatest percentage increase in expenditures has occurred in centralized research because of the large K-3 Project launched a few years ago. This trend will continue. The allocation has grown from $5,000 to $11,000 in the past four years.

Let us now talk about supporting services which have some feature or aspect that can be recognized as being a recent addition to services normally found in public school systems.

**Establishing and operating a district-wide instructional
planning center (including a curriculum materials center,
audio-visual production and circulation center, print shop,
professional library, and work stations)**

In our district those services (function #2) necessary for the
development of instructional plans and those (function #3) that
facilitate the effective implementation of new programs and/or
materials were brought together physically and functionally when
we created the Ladue Instructional Planning Center in 1966. Prior
to that time each of the separate services was being up-graded
on an individual basis.

Reprinted here are descriptions of the more important objectives and operational systems of the Ladue Instructional Planning
Center. These were taken from a memo distributed to administrators
and coordinators during the second year of the center's operation.
The objectives and systems are grouped according to the three main
functions of the center: *in-service, production,* and *circulation.*

Objectives of the Instructional Planning Center	Operational Systems to Accomplish Objectives
IN SERVICE	
(I.P.C. Director)	
Promote with principals, librarians, and teachers the development of IPC capacities in the individual buildings.	Survey status of "IPC" capacities throughout the district by visiting individual buildings. Assist principals and interested teachers in projecting desirable increased capacities.
Promote utilization of IPC services and products.	Distribute and maintain the *IPC Reference Guide.* Distribute periodic newsletter announcing new materials and encouraging utilization of IPC services.

Objectives of the Instructional Planning Center	Operational Systems to Accomplish Objectives
Refer production to agencies outside the center when advisable.	Establish contacts with area printers and AV centers. Encourage cooperative arrangements with neighboring school districts and colleges. Secure cost estimates for products of unusual quality or format beyond the capacity of the IPC.
Involve and assist principals in planning in-service programs for teachers.	Invite principals to ask for services of IPC in planning and conducting in-service for staff. Secure out-of-district consultants through Coordinator of Instruction. Encourage scheduling of in-service in facilities of IPC.
Demonstrate the use of new methods and materials.	Arrange demonstrations of commercial materials by suppliers. Arrange demonstrations by teachers in pilot projects. Make and use video tape recordings of pilot classes.
Develop a system of instructional planning and assist teachers and principals in the use of systematic instructional planning for lessons, units, and courses.	Formulate sets of objectives (written in terms of student behavior), criterion tests, and classroom activities which project an effective, sequential package of precise and cohesive developmental tasks directed toward changing the capacities and dispositions of students in some desirable way. (See flow chart in Chapter Two.)
Advise in the design of pilot programs, courses, units, lessons, and supplementary materials.	Identify and encourage potential authors to apply for IPC-sponsored projects with ultimate approval of the IPC Executive

Objectives of the Instructional Planning Center	Operational Systems to Accomplish Objectives
	Committee. Advise and assist authors in the final production of the materials, including instructions to users.
Schedule and coordinate typing of master copy for products.	Whenever possible, have usable camera-ready copy produced by authors or secretaries in their individual buildings. —or— Secure legible rough draft copy with specific instructions regarding format. Establish reasonable deadlines. Facilitate in any way possible the cooperative effort between authors and typists.
Evaluate the relationship of program elements to instructional outcomes with the assistance of the Director of Research, School Psychologist, principals, and teachers.	Have evaluator confer with authors to agree upon (1) the changes in attitudes, knowledge, and skills to be measured and (2) the research design and procedures to be employed in the study. Assist evaluator in the production of evaluation instruments. Coordinate efforts of administrators, teachers, counselors, Director of Research, and Psychologist in conducting the study. Conduct studies for several years as needed.
Participate in the preparation and execution of public relations efforts of the schools.	Report newsworthy projects to Director of Public Relations. Assist P. R. Director in collection and formulation of news items. Assist in the design of supporting AV materials for major presentations.

Objectives of the Instructional Planning Center	Operational Systems to Accomplish Objectives
Participate in the orientation of new staff.	Prepare special announcement and invitation for new staff encouraging them to use services of IPC. Have special orientation sessions in IPC for new staff with focus on production and use of AV materials.

PRODUCTION

(Coordinator of Multi-Media)

Schedule and coordinate production in the print shop.	Devise receiving system for all duplicating and printing jobs so that jobs will be done either immediately or assigned a priority position in the printer's work schedule. All instructions needed by the printer should be written on the work order. Recommend that production be done at local school when the situation warrants this. Maintain a monthly work schedule for all monthly and annual productions or have a visual inventory to signal need for rerun of consumable forms and notices. Assist printer in securing necessary supplies for projected production, printing and binding.
Advise and assist staff with the format and design of instructional materials, including the drawing of illustrations.	Author and artist confer to agree upon the over-all effect that material is to have. Basic agreement is reached about text and illustration (if any) per page and basic margins and openness of copy. Preliminary sketches and

Objectives of the Instructional Planning Center	Operational Systems to Accomplish Objectives
	layouts will be pasted up and checked by author if necessary. Artist will make search for accurate visual portrayals when needed and not supplied by the author.
Recommend most appropriate packaging of materials for projected instructional activities.	Author and IPC staff will select the most appropriate packaging or binding for the materials, giving consideration to nature of use, for how long, by whom. IPC staff will continue to increase the number of ways it can package and bind materials.
Produce first edition of locally prepared materials.	IPC Director, production head, and authors will project a detailed production work schedule specifying the number of each printout, type, size and color of stock, ink color, one or two side print, instructions for collating, punching, and binding. Distribution will be spelled out and shipping date set. All master copies should be filed in IPC for future use, along with a copy production work schedule.
Reproduce materials for wider distribution or continued use.	Second requests should be filled from inventory if possible. Using master copy or good quality first copy make Bruning masters for second run. Authors and IPC staff determine size of run to meet immediate request and to maintain a reasonable inventory for anticipated future requests.

Objectives of the Instructional Planning Center	Operational Systems to Accomplish Objectives
	Each spring a survey of users should be made to firm up estimates of future requests.
Produce 35 mm slides and overhead transparencies.	Upon receipt of selected references and/or rough sketches, the artist will prepare *35mm slides* or *overhead transparencies* at the direction of the requestee. On-location photographic work will also be done upon request. Detailed instructions regarding text, illustrations, layout, and overlays must be agreed upon in the case of transparencies. When advisable and possible, instructions will be given to enable teachers to make their own transparencies and slides with equipment at their school.
Produce audio and video tapes.	Audio tapes will be produced from script, records, sound tracks, other tapes, or any combination of these. A blank tape should be supplied by the requestee if at all possible. On-location video tapes will be made by the IPC staff or by local staff trained by the IPC staff. Video tapes will be held only for one or two days except for special situations. Individual buildings should be encouraged to purchase their own inventory of ½ inch video tapes.
Laminate flat graphics to extend usability.	Master copy for making transparencies will be preserved by

Objectives of the Instructional Planning Center	Operational Systems to Accomplish Objectives
	lamination. Single page printed material, drawings, etc., not exceeding 11″ in width, may be preserved with thin lamination or be made rigid with thick lamination. Use of material should determine type of lamination.
Select and maintain production equipment.	Maintain contact with suppliers of production equipment. Employ service contracts or on-call service to maintain equipment in top working condition. Attend exhibits and demonstrations by suppliers. Arrange trial uses of new equipment when necessary. Coordinator of Multi-Media will recommend purchases of equipment to Coordinator of Instruction.
Operate a loan schedule of audio-visual equipment for presentation and production by staff outside the IPC.	Establish and operate procedures for reserving, signing out, delivering, operating, returning, and checking in special audio-visual equipment for use by anyone outside the Center, including other staff in the Board of Education or anywhere in the district.
Select and maintain an inventory of supplies.	Maintain contact with suppliers of audio-visual and paper supplies. Establish and maintain an adequate inventory, storing materials either in the IPC, the Print Shop, or the warehouse. When possible secure supplies from or charge supplies to individual buildings.

Objectives of the Instructional Planning Center	Operational Systems to Accomplish Objectives
Demonstrate varied and optimum use of audio-visual equipment.	Hold demonstrations in IPC and in individual buildings upon request. Hold training sessions with individual operators as needed. (Many more of these are being held now.)

CIRCULATION

(Secretary of Materials Center)

Search available resources in response to specific request for staff.	Staff may request service by phone, note, or by visit to IPC. All materials should be labeled and shelved systematically in such a way as to be directly accessible by visiting staff as well as IPC staff. The circulation system should include simple procedures for reserving, checking out, delivery, return deadlines, checking in, and reshelving.
Maintain a current collection of published texts and teaching materials.	Maintain contact with coordinators, principals, librarians, and teachers to identify materials that should be available in Materials Center. Ask salesmen to keep the sampling of their materials comprehensive and up to date. Search exhibits and journals for identification of new materials.
Maintain files on sources of commercially prepared materials.	Maintain catalogue file by company and advertisement file by subject and/or media. Make compilations of and indexes to instructional materials available in the Materials Center and the Professional Library.

Objectives of the Instructional Planning Center	Operational Systems to Accomplish Objectives
Maintain a professional library.	IPC staff upon recommendation of administrators, coordinators, teachers, and special staff will secure, process, and circulate professional books, journals, pamphlets, out-of-district curriculum guides, national experimental programs, and selected professional newsletters. Secretaries to the Coordinators will assist staff in use of the Professional Library.
Advise local building staffs regarding the processing and circulation of instructional materials.	IPC staff will assist librarians and principals in improving the organization and operation of materials centers in their buildings for teachers and for students.
Disseminate information about new methods and materials.	Produce a newsletter that reports successful uses of new methods and materials in the district and that identifies items recently added to materials center which teachers might want to try.
Recommend selected commerical materials for consideration by appropriate staff.	Complex 3-dimensional kits, sets of books, etc., would be packaged for circulation to schools and/or individual staff members who had indicated some interest. Loan of such materials would be made by suppliers to the IPC for a given length of time for promotional purposes.
Schedule and arrange sessions for screening promising new instructional materials.	Relay announcement of new AV materials to selected staff. Arrange for screening to be done in the IPC or for materials to be scheduled and sent to interested

Objectives of the Instructional Planning Center	Operational Systems to Accomplish Objectives
	person for screening outside IPC. Assist St. Louis County Audio-Visual Dept. and KETC educational channel in promoting the use of their materials and programs.

The several *summer* IPC projects of 1970 were described at the end of Chapter Two to give a specific picture of the activities in and around the center during the summer months. Between September and June there is a steady flow of services consisting of equal amounts of in-service, production, and circulation activities as described above. New instructional programs in social studies, sex education, and drug abuse education rely heavily on a sizable flow of correlated audio-visual materials circulated out of the IPC. Such activity is reminiscent of city audio-visual departments of former days. However, in our situation the materials are items purchased or developed specifically as an integral part of instructional packages produced by our teachers for the Ladue curriculum.

Applications for sponsored summer projects are submitted between January and April each year. The IPC Executive Committee, made up of the central office administrators, three secondary principals, three elementary principals, and the Coordinator of Instruction, review the applications and make recommendations to the Administrative Council, which gives final approval or makes other dispositions of the proposals. In the case of approved projects, the Coordinator of Multi-Media makes detailed arrangements with the successful applicants regarding work stations and work schedule. He also assigns a central office coordinator to act as continuing liaison agent between the project team and the IPC staff. The sponsored applicants are paid supplementary summer salaries equivalent to those received by staff working in summer school or summer recreation. A detailed description of the support given to summer teams by the IPC staff can be found in the middle of Chapter Two.

At the present time the greatest expansion of IPC services is in the production of audio-visual materials. Transparencies of high quality are printed by a Thermofax or Technifax system, using master copy with lettering from the Varityper Headliner and drawings by the Multi-Media Coordinator.

The Coordinator of Visual Arts and the Coordinator of Multi-Media continue to conduct workshops in which they demonstrate materials and techniques the regular classroom teacher can use to produce his own teaching aids. New sheets of press-on lettering and color acetate made by Letraset have provided an easy way for the untalented and unskilled practitioner to make effective, high quality visuals. The two 35mm slide cameras and the Bolex super 8mm movie camera of the IPC are used very regularly for slide-making and film-making. Individual staff members and student crews in all of our elementary and secondary schools have become proficient in using one or more of our portable ½ inch video taping systems.

Other departments and buildings are gradually acquiring their own equipment to allow student production of audio-visual reports in academic areas as well as special presentations in fine arts. Student-made slides were used in the recent staging of an elementary assembly to provide dynamic backdrops for youthful songsters rendering a combination of new and old holiday tunes.

The print shop has grown from a mimeograph machine to two offset presses, an electrostatic master maker, an automatic 12 bin collator, a folder, a paper punch drill, light and heavy stapler, a plastic spiral punch and binder, heavy duty paper cutter, and a 120-page booklet folder designed and made by our master printer. Other minor pieces of equipment and procedures are employed to handle a long, utilitarian array of printed forms and publications for the district. There is only an occasional printing job that goes beyond our composing capabilities or our printout sizes. A well-trained senior printer and a full-time assistant printer are the invaluable operators of our print shop. The skill and care they apply to their work makes an unbelievable difference in the end product as compared to what other operators turn out on the same equipment.

The secretary of the IPC processes and circulates all printed and audio-visual materials stored in the 15' by 30' shelf-lined materials center. As indicated earlier, multiple sets of correlated audio-visual materials (purchased as well as locally produced) make it possible for long term loans of these materials. Teachers are asked to reserve materials in advance if possible. With an early indication of demand, slight adjustments in schedule or sharing of materials within a building can be suggested so that all teachers' needs are met. More expensive simulations and games are also circulated under the same arrangements.

The secretary to the Coordinator of Instruction is librarian for the professional library, since it is located adjacent to her station. Two trained librarians organized the basic collection on a Dewey Decimal system. Now, the Coordinator of Instruction and his secretary handle ordering, processing, and circulation of all new books without specialized help. The proper coding of materials can be done by any person knowledgeable about the contents of the selections by using coding of categories already established in the library. For a specialized library, this type of coding will group together quite appropriately all types of material you are likely to want in your special collection. A complete card catalogue is maintained, listing all items by author, title, and one or more subjects. Parents as well as staff members are welcomed to call in requests or to visit the library whenever it is not being used for a meeting.

During the summer, the library is a highly prized silent work area for individuals and groups doing reading or writing in conjunction with some curriculum planning. Other school libraries throughout the district are also used as work stations for summer IPC-sponsored groups, since appropriate work areas become very limited in the center itself. The center is fully occupied with audio-visual and print production.

Reference materials which the teams wish are ordered through the professional library. Some items are returned for shelving in the library. Others are purchased in sufficient numbers for distribution in the teachers' kits accompanying the newly produced instructional units.

In many instances, references requested are available through public and university libraries in our area. Such books are borrowed through our professional library for the specific time period requested by the production teams. Sometimes we secure photostated copies of pages of references or periodicals which cannot be removed from the outside libraries. Tapping these community sources in this fashion actually makes our library services equivalent to the best a metropolitan area can offer.

We use the requests of staff members to identify what items should be added to our professional collection. It is a common occurrence for administrators, coordinators, or teachers to recommend a teacher reference which they think would improve the implementation of some aspect of our on-going program or some projected part of an in-service session. In such instances multiple copies are ordered and distributed to appropriate staff, with one copy processed for the library.

The Teachers' Library, published by the NEA in 1968, was helpful that year in reviewing the comprehensiveness and balance of our collection. A special supplementary purchase of books listed in that reference served to round out our collection. The problem, as would be expected, is to manage an adequate program of new purchases, replacements, and culling out to live within forty-two shelf sections available.

Three other features of the professional library are worthy of mention. First, there is a collection of forty professional periodicals deposited on magazine racks after they have been circulated through a prearranged route as per the requests of administrators, coordinators, and principals. This service supplements what they order for their own buildings.

Another special collection is called the pamphlet file. Like most such files, this collection contains small publications on special topics, dated reports that will serve only one or two years, and other items judged unworthy for full processing. The file is maintained according to a subject index. The librarian keeps a dated listing as her control of pamphlet and magazine circulation. There is a regular card signout system for all materials in the main library and the materials center.

The collection of curriculum guides from our district and from selected others is the final feature of our library to be mentioned here. Processing copies of all Ladue teacher's guides and placing them in the library makes them available for lay persons as well as staff. Candidates for the board of education have made good use of this collection.

"Creating" new supporting services through cooperation between the community and the school

More extensive and functional use of lay and professional resources outside the school can constitute a most valuable form of additional services to curriculum renewal.

It now appears that the school's traditional use of community and professional resources is going to experience a metamorphosis in the very near future. A more extended discussion of this possible trend may be found in Chapter Seven. Even under present arrangements, the use of outside resources constitutes important support to both the development of new programs and the enrichment of established studies.

During the past few years special personnel of the city art museum, the museum of science and natural history, the regional telephone company, and the local educational television channel have assisted us in our revision of instructional programs. In each instance persons either conducted workshops for staff or provided special field-trip experiences as one of the student activities in the revised curriculum.

With the returning view of education as a function of the total community, we along with all school districts will be developing means other than the field trip or the invited resource person as ways for using the community. We will move toward direct involvement of teachers and students in the on-going life of the immediate community.

We have in mind more realistic investigations of adult organizations and activities than is possible through the guest speaker, the taped telephone interview, or the field trip. We will be particularly interested in the educational services maintained by all public agencies and private enterprises, those designed to train their personnel and those designed to educate potential customers about the value and nature of their goods and services. Students would be helped in comprehending what is required for the care and feeding of a community. New "open schools" such as the Parkway program in Philadelphia have taken the study of the community as the basic rationale and framework for organizing its entire curriculum.

While we are moving toward such radical departures, we will continue to draw on the materials and services of the public libraries, public transportation, public health departments, city hall, the post office, highway departments, police, firemen, local business, and industry to confront students with aspects of community life.

The participation of staff in graduate programs offered in area universities and colleges will continue to be a major opportunity for professional growth. Master of Arts in Teaching in special subject areas as offered by Webster College seems to be effective in causing teachers to make a serious re-examination of methods and materials for educating the young. Insights and skills gained from such exploratory approaches to curriculum construction and teaching have contributed visibly to the products of our instructional teams. Teaching styles of individual teachers have also been affected.

We have found that participation in regional curriculum projects such as those of the St. Louis County Social Studies Center, the Madison Project, and the Midwest Regional Educational Laboratory does upgrade our staff members' skills in curriculum design and production. These projects also supply alternative instructional units to our staff and students. One unique effect of such curriculum laboratories is that they keep local practitioners aware of new strategies and materials emerging across the nation and beyond. One problem with the educational laboratory is that it has no marketing system for its products. That is a function local districts must perform.

A university-level experience, whether brought to the local school or taken on campus, is essential for improving the leadership skills of all neophyte curriculum coordinators. Therefore, an important support to curriculum renewal is the encouragement that a school district provides to its staff to continue graduate study. Studies making an intense investigation of methods and content of a particular subject are most applicable. However, refreshers in learning theory and educational philosophy are equally good in broadening the practitioner's perspective of the whole task of instructional planning.

It is my present opinion that laboratory experiences in lesson planning and curriculum construction (see Triple T of Chapter

Seven) are more productive of the skills of the curriculum planner than general courses in curriculum theory. Members of our staff have been privileged to participate in such curriculum projects as the Family Finance Institute, the Madison Project, the Carnegie Social Studies Project, and the Elementary Science Studies. We consider the projects we do locally as very authentic experiences in curriculum planning, though on a smaller scale and addressed only to the needs of our students.

SEVEN

Responding to
social and
educational issues
with new insights
and technology

Something of great import has been missing in this book up to this point. You should be drummed out of the corps if you were not troubled by its absence. That something was the relevance of curriculum planning to some concept of the needs of man and society.

Finally, therefore, we must face the ultimate question: "Curriculum renewal for what?"

Joyce of Teachers College, Columbia University, avers that our curriculum planning today is geared toward offering learning environments in which youth can acquire personal and technical proficiencies needed to move up the status hierarchy of our existing society. In other words, he is saying that many, if not all, curriculum workers hold this final goal for their efforts. Holding to such an objective, curriculum workers assume that they add stars to their crowns whenever their instructional changes improve the school's efficiency in producing proficient, status-seeking technocrats.

Joyce's thesis, as expressed in the final chapter of the 1971 NSSE Yearbook, is that little if any *significantly needed* curriculum change will be invented by practitioners confined to such a narrow, society-oriented educational goal.

What if one chooses more humanistic ends for education? What if the school's goal, unlike that of a large majority in our society, is to help youngsters discover and actualize themselves as individuals and explore the creative possibilities in interaction with others? Can a curriculum worker have goals which are different from the expectations of our present society? And with such goals, can curriculum renewal to him mean the *creation of entirely new institutional environments* for the education of the young?

It is my belief that holding such expectations for education is the mark of real educational leadership.

Setting our sights on a more humanistic education

It is my desire that curriculum renewal be oriented toward humanistic transactions which may heal some of the personal disorders and social ills of mankind. I believe that personal and social fulfillment can be a more common condition among the peoples of our earth.

Under the umbrella of humanistic goals we must commit ourselves to a great array of *particular* educational missions, to be implemented through an equally great array of learning environments—learning environments that facilitate experiences of personal affirmation, group therapy, social awareness, academic inquiry, and scientific experimentation, to list just a few.

In the remainder of this chapter, I shall cite for your consideration a few of the encouraging signs which I believe indicate that both the process and the products of curriculum planning are tending toward more humanistic goals.

Here are some questions which might help us detect what humanistic trends exist in today's curriculum planning.

Are we thinking again in terms of whole, unique persons? Are we striving again for a more sensitive adult interacting compassionately with responsive, developing youngsters? Are we accepting differences and giving learners individual, optional, direct access to varied environments? Are students and teachers being helped to know peak human experiences through the exercise of their feelings, imaginations, and social skills? Do more persons share in the process of curriculum renewal with curriculum decision-making spread throughout the institutional system? Are students and teachers held responsible for larger blocks of time and expanded territory for exploration? Is there increased professionalism in the training of teachers? Has research and inventiveness filled the teacher's kit with additional effective, exciting alternatives? Has technology been harnessed to carry more of the repetitious, mundane chores of education? Has technology been made the servant of education rather than its goal?

Thinking again of the whole child and the whole society

Curriculum planners, be they students, teachers, principals, coordinators, or parents, must take the larger, humanistic view. This means a commitment to the importance and uniqueness of each person and an acceptance of the pluralism, interdependence, and integrity of all societies and the physical environments in which they live.

One general goal must be to encourage learning styles which fully activate the curiosity and compassion of the human spirit. A companion goal must be to develop institutional forms, including involvements in the larger community, which will embody such learning styles as a way of life for our times. An underlying assumption is that institutions cannot change unless persons in them change first.

Citation One: The Free School Movement began in the late sixties, basing its philosophy on the British Infant School concept. In a recent *IPI News Notes*, the free school movement was reported as being a rapidly growing enterprise, at that time there being an estimated two thousand such schools all over the U.S. and Canada. The teacher of one such school said: ''Play is the natural work of the child. Kids learn by playing. We give these kids the liberty to learn when they're good and ready to.''

Citation Two: In a recent announcement, the St. Louis City Schools reported that the open classroom concept will be explored by an elementary teacher on special assignment to the New City School. In addition to her work at the school, she will work with supervisory staffs of the five districts and with any school staff wishing her services.

Citation Three: By the end of the first semester last year, an experienced first grade teacher invited me to visit her "informal" classroom. Except for an opening class discussion about what the day might have in store for certain individuals and groups (each received his "active" work folder), each of those six-year-olds went his own way the rest of the day, choosing to be in the living-room library, the filmstrip and record section, the science laboratory corner, the play bin of large blocks, the tables with cuisennaire rods and other mathematical objects, the arts and crafts section, or the reading corner where the teacher was available to assist with reading skills of individuals or small groups not exceeding three at a time. The happy, relaxed, responsible behavior of the children was a joy to behold. The most impressive thing was the way they worked out their own squabbles over materials, equipment, or space. The teacher reported that learning to handle their own conflicts took the greater portion of the children's and teacher's energy during the first semester.

Citation Four: With parent conferences being held during the first quarter with parents of all elementary students in our district, we are moving toward a system of reporting to parents which will consist of two conferences and two brief written reports each year. These will focus more on how well each child is coping with the total demands of life at school than on his specific standing in each academic skill. Children will be present during part of many of these parent conferences.

Sensitizing staff to human transactions

In our district we call it humanizing the school. District-wide attention has been given to identifying the personal traits and teaching techniques which seem to increase the staff member's rapport with students of different age groups and which cause youngsters to feel good about themselves and their experiences at school. A useful resource in this endeavor has been a doctoral study completed by our former Assistant Coordinator of Instruction, describing several experimental methods in motivation to change self concept in students.

Citation Five: A small group of volunteer high school teachers continue to conduct open discussion sessions on the book, *I'm OK, You're OK,* by Harris. This book and these sessions are rated very understandable and useful by teachers as they seek improved self-understanding and greater insight into the behavior of their students. Transactional analysis as discussed in this book confronts the individual with the fact that he is responsible for what happens in the future, no matter what has happened in the past. Harris postulates the absolute necessity of a system of moral values if individuals and a society are to survive. He quotes Nathaniel Branden as saying: "Effective psychotherapy requires a conscious, rational, scientific code of ethics—a system of values based on the facts of reality and geared to the needs of man's life on earth."

Citation Six: We also had surprisingly good success with a one-and-a-half-day workshop on small group techniques. Our high school English teachers had requested such a session because they did not feel satisfied with either teacher or student performance in twice-a-week small group seminars. Dr. John Schultz, then chairman of the counseling department at the University of Missouri at St. Louis, worked with our Director of Special Services and our Coordinator of Language Arts as the leadership team for those sessions. The sensitivity experiences were effective in exposing the teachers' diverse attitudes and role expectations with regard to the seminar situation.

At the end of the workshop, teachers acknowledged that they had acquired keener insight into themselves and a new appreciation of the potential of the seminar as a learning environment. Teachers also discussed the possibility that their feelings and those of their students might be causing some of the disappointing behaviors seen in the seminars. To that extent, that particular use of sensitivity training seemed to have proved appropriate for staff development. However, the teachers requested further help in modifying their own behavior toward becoming more effective seminar teachers.

A planning committee of English teachers met with the Coordinator of Language Arts, the Coordinator of Guidance, the Director of Special Services, and the Coordinator of Instruction to devise some follow-up sessions. Actually, prior to the meeting of this large planning group, the Coordinator of Language Arts and the Chariman of the English Department had outlined what appeared to them to be promising approaches. Then at the meeting of the total planning committee it was decided that during a concentrated one-week schedule, the four coordinators would visit seminars to identify what seemed to be their greatest strength as a teaching-learning strategy. We coordinators were then scheduled to report our findings to the entire English department the following Monday.

As would be expected, during our visitations we saw what we considered weaknesses as well as strengths. But true to our "sensitivity oriented" plan, we confined our report to highlighting exemplary performances on the part of teachers and students, and commented generally upon the positive features which seemed to characterize an effective seminar. The report session adjourned with some teachers probing us for more frank criticism of what we had seen. However, we kept our lips well buttoned and gradually departed. Upon revisiting the school later in the week, we happily learned that the English teachers genuinely appreciated what we had said and that they welcomed our periodic observation of seminars as well as other sessions, such as individual conferences or large group sessions.

It appeared that we had achieved a rapport with this group which would allow us to function as friendly mirrors, reflecting to them in a helpful way another perspective of their operations. Another apparent effect of our particular and limited use of sensitivity training techniques seemed to have been the improved human relations among English teachers, as well as between teachers and students. I would see more use of this approach for the improvement of instruction in our school district in the future.

Citation Seven: Our High School Instructional Council, after spending several sessions on how we might humanize our high school, appointed a subcommittee to contact students and parents about the matter. A meeting of the subcommittee with fifteen students and fifteen parents produced twenty-four suggested approaches, such as, organize a Big Brother organization, develop curriculum improvements in vocational training, improve race relations and police relations by improved communication and contact, open campus, and have a group of students on the faculty council. Only as the Instructional Council continues its interaction with these groups will we know the impact of these efforts.

Accepting individual differences

IPI and other means for effective individualization will be an integral part of future educational services. With packaging such as IPI it will be possible for these services to be offered any place convenient to the consumer: the school, the library, the church, the community center, or the home. Service-oriented technicians would be adequate to give clerical guidance and personal support to individual learners, as well as issue certificates indicating satisfactory completion of designated sections of the programs.

Citation Eight: A report of the Vermont State Design for Education included seventeen premises as an ideal philosophy for individualizing instruction. Permit me to list a few of these to point up the common base of individualized instruction and humanistic education: "1. The emphasis must be upon learning, rather than teaching. 2. A student must be accepted as a person. . . . 6. Emphasis should be upon a child's own way of learning. . . . 10. The teacher's role must be that of a partner and guide in the learning process. . . . 13. The environment within which students are encouraged to learn must be greatly expanded."

Citation Nine: Project Upswing will train volunteers to help children in the first year of the ungraded primary. Volunteers will work with the pupils on a one-to-one basis. The training program will begin in the fall. The project is a cooperative venture of the St. Louis Public Schools and the University of Missouri at St. Louis.

Citation Ten: A recent *IPI News Notes* carried the following announcement regarding Hampshire College in Amherst, Massachusetts: "Once enrolled on campus, students advance at their own pace through a carefully established sequence of divisions of study. . . . Under this plan, the student may complete his degree in three, four, or more years."

Citation Eleven: During the last year in our district the number of primary teachers with individualized reading programs went from four to sixteen. This expansion was due to a combination of the expanded variety of commercial materials and systems that have become available for individualizing reading, plus promotion through in-service by our Coordinator of Language Arts assisted by teachers.

Citation Twelve: Our high school teacher of business information and data processing recently purchased sets (five per student) of programmed texts so that some students could move quickly to hands-on experience with the key punch while others maintained a slower pace.

Exercising one's own feelings, imagination, reason, and social skills

New social studies programs involve youngsters in role playing, gaming, and simulations. Such experiences help the student appreciate the feelings and different points of view of persons in the historical events or social controversies being studied. The student's rational powers for clarifying values and social skills for seeking compromises are also refined when he applies them in simulated social conflicts, either historical or contemporary.

Citation Thirteen: In St. Louis the CECH Program (Citizenship Education Clearing House) will give students in social studies classes actual experiences in citizenship by working in the community on elections, pollution, environmental controls, etc. Schools participating are Cleveland, Southwest, and Soldan High Schools.

Citation Fourteen: It can be made as a general statement that audio-visual productions by students are becoming informative, exciting learning experiences in modern schools.

In our district, the Multi-Media Coordinator and the Coordinator of Visual Arts are facilitating the production of student AV reports and AV art forms. Automatic features in new photographic equipment have greatly improved the products of teachers and students.

A great array of classroom efforts comes to mind. New life was injected into an apathetic, nonachieving group of eighth graders when the teacher proposed that they make a short film. Language arts skills were dusted off and used in the preparation of a script revolving about a classroom incident of a disastrous trick played on an unsuspecting teacher. Technical problems were encountered in providing adequate inside lighting. Clothing changes by actors during the week of shooting slightly spoiled the illusion of the one-day sequences in the film. Nevertheless, the automatic 8mm Bolex camera did its job well, and the accompanying student-produced tape inserted a respectable measure of suspense. The student acting was excellent in several instances.

The big payoff was the lift in class pride and individual self-respect that came from having accomplished well what no other group in that school had done up to that point. The presentation was shown to parents as well as to interested classes. The teacher was elated with the product and with the positive change in class behaviors and attitudes. Her only criticism was that the twenty-five-minute film was five times too long. Her recommendation was that a five- to ten-minute film would have achieved the same effects with much less stress and strain on all concerned. The editing process was the champion consumer of time and energy. Consequently, regarding this aspect, she recommended that in the future, scenes be shot initially in their proper sequence. This would minimize the editing as well as eliminate some of the problems with changes in dress.

Citation Fifteen: Animated films may be a most appropriate project for all ages. It can call forth all kinds of creativity from students and teachers, while at the same time avoiding some of the more complicated and laborious feats of live film-making. The antics of figurines and cut paper dolls can intrigue the young and old when brought to life through the single frame magic of a firmly mounted 8mm movie camera.

Art teachers in our district, under the tutelage of our Coordinator of Visual Arts, are beginning to make animated films in their own classes and are assisting regular teachers in conducting such projects as an aspect of the academic curriculum. Below, you will find an excerpt from an instructional memo from one of our art teachers to our staff about her work with three elementary students in producing an animated film.

ANIMATION

To be *animate* is to be alive. To be *inanimate* is to lack life and spirit. *Animation* is the special act of giving life and spirit to the inanimate; an act that transforms tag board and paint into movement and life.

The total effort of animation encompassed many varied disciplines. The young people, the animators played many roles. . . . story writer, artist, director of film movement and life, film editor, sound director, and voice actors. In my experimental work in animation, I was very fortunate to have worked with three very creative young people. When I lacked a knowledge of any one of the disciplines necessary to the animation, the young people were intelligent enough to make up for my lack of guidance.

Because of the variety of disciplines involved in the process of animation, it is my opinion that any large group effort in animation should be guided by a team of staff members rather than just the art staff. The classroom teacher would be an excellent guide in the literary and mathematical aspects of animation. The music staff would be the most suitable choice to guide the sound efforts. The art staff would give guidance in all the visual aspects of the animation effort.

Citation Sixteen: Inexpensive hand-mounted as well as commercially processed 35mm color slides offer an easier means for students and teachers to create their own audio-visual presentations. In the primary grades, impressive topical reports can be made by the very young out of transparent contact lifts of pictures and print from magazines printed on clay-based paper.

In the upper elementary and secondary grades, multiple audio tapes provide a conceptual base for simultaneous multiple projection of slides. Impelling descriptive and psychedelic effects can be achieved. One such junior high project shown to fifty visiting art educators displayed a dramatic mixture of Thermofax-produced black and white slides amidst contact lifts and experimental "chemical" slides, the latter being the mounting of any transparent resins and paints. One script was a moving, free form type poetry written by an eighth grade girl. The unique characteristic of such presentations is that the variations are limitless, especially when further modified by the rhythmic movement of the slides, pulsing of the zoom lens, and gradual dim-outs through slow "shuttering" with the hand. The content may run from serious nonfictional commentary to formless, unintelligible musical and verbal nonsense. All sorts of purposes may be served, the most common being the opportunity for students to express themselves in the multi-media age.

Citation Seventeen: For a final report of AV production by students, let me reprint a news item from the winter issue of one of our elementary school's student newspaper.

SLIDES

In Social Studies, the fourth grades have been studying about friendly and unfriendly behavior. We made slides illustrating these kinds of behavior. This is the way we did it.

First you need a lot of magazines from which to choose pictures. Take a slide mount and trace around the inside of it on the picture. Place a piece of clear contact paper over the part of the picture you want. Cut it out and trim it to fit the mount. Soak this picture in water until you can pull the picture off. After you have the paper off, wash it in water to remove all the paper content. Place it on a paper towel, sticky side up. When it is dry, put it on a smooth baggie, sticky side down, and trim it to correct size. Fit it in the slide mount and press.

Each person in our class made six slides. We showed them in the projector to choose the ones we thought best to use. Our tape will soon be ready to share with the other class.

Mrs. (fourth grade teacher)'s class has finished their project and they showed them to our room. We enjoyed seeing them. Dr. Morley and Mr. (principal) were guests.

Distributing decision-making throughout the institutional system

Decision-making may be distributed throughout an institutional system in at least three basic ways. First, upper members of a hierarchy can make a special effort to communicate with members of other levels before they make final policy decisions. Such two-way communication will assure a more informed and compassionate base for the decision, as well as increase the understanding and acceptance by those affected by the decisions.

Second, upper members of a hierarchy can delegate specific areas of decision-making to those below them. The risk for the leader in delegating power to others is knowing that if anything goes wrong, he will still be held responsible for how the lower echelon used that power.

Third, members who share some delegated decision-making responsibility at a particular level can use a consensus type procedure for widest possible involvement of persons at that level. Obviously, such broad involvement plus a consensus approach will assure maximum support of the agreed-upon plan by the peer group.

Citation Eighteen: A recent *Education Turnkey News* had an item by a specialist in educational technology who said that the basic ideas of performance contracting should provide school districts with a managerial model for making optimum use of innovative technology with minimized adverse effect on staff development and curriculum improvement.

If an outside agency can work with a school's teachers and achieve a significant improvement in student performance, why can't the school's instructional specialist do the same thing? It seems realistic to predict that either the central office staff will find ways to accomplish improved student performance, or they will and should be replaced by a private contractor.

Citation Nineteen: Given an instructional planning center such as ours, a logical application of in-house performance contracting would be to use such an arrangement as part of our summer contract with local production teams. In other words, a team applying for four weeks to revise the language arts program for a target group of students would be offered a basic supplementary salary for their summer production of plans and materials, with the possibility of a *bonus* supplementary salary if the target student population improved to a certain predetermined level in specific performances. The constraints, I feel sure, on doing this sort of thing would be numerous in a public school setting, but not insurmountable.

Citation Twenty: Carefully selected teacher-teams can produce and implement effective curriculum improvement. We have evidence that thoughtfully developed and well implemented locally produced materials can have measurable effect on student performance. I would cite one IPC project of two summers ago. Two seventh grade mathematics teachers worked a few weeks under the direction of the department chairman. They produced a 100-page folder of activity sheets which they thought would strengthen the computational and problem-solving skills of students. Our emphasis on modern math had increased students' insight into the structure of mathematics and the logic of its operations, but at some cost to their computational skills.

Here is the end of that story as reported to me by one of our junior high principals:

Ladue Junior High School
January 1971

Frank,

We scored!

The attached graph shows the gains, each year since 1965, which our 8th grade classes have made in Iowa Basics.

Ten months' gain is equivalent to one year's growth.

You will recall that our math people were disturbed with our students' basic arithmetic skills and so designed the new seventh grade math course which was taught to 7th graders last year. It is most gratifying to see the remarkable gain [thirteen months] for that class—as 8th graders this year. It would seem that they most certainly achieved their objective.

Reading gains remain the most consistent.

Our 8th grade class I.Q. scores have remained remarkably consistent.

Citation Twenty-one: In the St. Louis City Schools, Project EFFECT will give teachers and principals an expanded role in the planning and development of the instructional programs in their schools. Seven schools have volunteered and been selected for the study, which will cover a three-year period. Schools participating in the project are: Blow, Gundlach, Monroe, Mount Pleasant, Walnut Park, McKinley High, and STEP. Also in St. Louis, Project Model Schools will set up an elementary school in each of five districts to serve as the experimental school of that district. The staff will experiment with materials, innovative procedures, and organizational and curriculum changes in an attempt to find better ways to teach children. Schools in the project are: Grant, Oak Hill, and Pruitt.

Citation Twenty-two: The community school movement with decision-making powers in the hands of neighborhood lay persons is another bright spot. Such programs run in the evening, are staffed by volunteers or paid teachers, and are subsidized by local government and private contributions.

Citation Twenty-three: Within a local junior high school, twelve sections of seventh graders are organized in three divisions of four sections each. An interdiscipline team of four teachers is in charge of each division. Each division has flexible space equivalent to four classrooms and eight modules daily (about three and one half hours) in which to study the areas of mathematics, science, English, and social studies. Preliminary planning by the three teaching teams has set the curriculum framework and general goals for the year. Planning by each team and its students proceeds creatively within that framework during the year. Time schedules, methods, and materials are modified and invented by each division and section as they seek better ways to enable all students to achieve the agreed-upon goals plus other objectives that emerge during the process.

Citation Twenty-four: That same junior high is conducting six noncredit mini-courses this quarter (eighteen were offered) which students have selected to take during their independent study modules. It is projected that a set of such mini-courses will be offered each quarter throughout the year. Through the process of selection, the decision-making power rests in the hands of the students, the only constraints being conflicts in schedules. There are no prerequisites and no grades

Ranging to environments outside the school

Use of off-campus sites for learning now range from the traditional morning or afternoon field trip to a cruise around the world. A promising off-campus learning experience falling in between these two extremes is the arrangement for secondary students to work and study at stations in the community as an official part of their high school education.

Citation Twenty-five: A local high school permits seniors to act as teacher aides in their local elementary schools or to serve as tutors to inner city youngsters needing help with academic skills. Other more varied types of volunteer duty with community service agencies are also approved as a part of career exploration for seniors.

Citation Twenty-six: A recent announcement suggests that St. Louis City Schools are launching their own "Parkway" plan. Project METRO at St. Louis will design a school "without walls" for secondary students. About 150 students will have the entire city as their classrooms and the expertise of civic, political, and business leaders as their sources of information. The school will provide educational options, and the students will exercise control over educational goals and objectives.

Citation Twenty-seven: Public and private educational centers such as area planetariums, art museums, and science museums may well be joined by private centers for guaranteed learning of basic academic skills. Ivan Illich, in *Deschooling Schools*, describes the organization and operation of such centers. When such centers do exist, public school teachers more than ever will need to be managers of learning environments inside and *outside* the school when guiding the learning of future enrollees.

Professionalizing the training of teachers

We seem to be arriving at more effective mixtures of pre-service and in-service training of teachers. As indicated in the previous section, as early as the senior year in high school, possible teaching candidates are given opportunities to test out their interests and aptitudes as teacher aides or tutors.

The phenomenon of differentiated staffing has offered a similar pre-career pattern to the late-entering housewife. She starts as a volunteer helper in the library, moves to being an employed teacher's aide and finally, returns to college, passes the prescribed courses, and becomes a certified teacher.

Regular pre-service training of teachers quite frequently now includes a great variety of classroom training experiences conducted jointly by the university and the local schools. In a similar manner, teachers employed by the local school districts receive an improved variety of in-service professional experiences conducted jointly by the local schools and the university.

Citation Twenty-eight: The educators in Temple City (California) Schools have organized a system of differentiated staffing comprised of six major components which they feel help to humanize education in several specific ways: "enhance human dignity, encourage individual enterprise, promote diversity and greater productivity, recognize and reward individual differences, and share power, authority, recognition, and decision-making." The differentiated staffing at Temple City recognizes different roles (and salaries) as follows: artist teacher with expanded curriculum leadership roles, senior teachers as subject area specialists who along with the principal make up the academic senate of each school, and paraprofessional aides who assist in operating a variety of lab stations and resource centers.

Citation Twenty-nine: The so-called Triple T program provides additional evidence that the trend will be toward the intimate intermixing of professional growth with on-going classroom experience. Triple T is a pre-service training arrangement which places administrators, trainers of teachers, experienced teachers, teachers in training, and school youngsters all together in a given operational situation. The designers of this teacher training arrangement intend that conceptual, attitudinal, and skill gains will accrue to all parties involved. It is my opinion that the potential is there for this to occur under good conditions.

One of the most effective techniques used by Triple T is the separate video tapings of mini-lessons taught by the teacher in training, the experienced teacher, and the university trainer of teachers. The follow-up viewing and frank critique of such sessions is good therapy for all three.

Equally valuable is their improved execution of such basic teacher behaviors as the delayed response, the reflected question, and the like. The building principal plays a legitimate and important role by exerting the proper control and support for what rapidly becomes a complex process of cooperative planning, cooperative execution, and cooperative critique, with a concluding item of preliminary planning for the next round of the training cycle.

As a research adjunct to the Triple T program in our schools,

Dr. Bryce Hudgins of Washington University has videotaped many hours of instruction by three experienced teachers in one of our elementary schools. A classroom has been converted into a studio where each of these teachers periodically takes his class for a forty-five minute taping session. The teachers, as directed, preplan three types of teaching: "particular"—the teaching of facts; "interpreting"—the search for some reasoned explanation of facts; and "concept"—the abstracting of unique characteristics that identify a worthwhile aspect of phenomena under study. With careful editing of these tapes, Dr. Hudgins has been able to display for the novice teacher (or the more expert) the essential ingredients of these three types of teaching. This input has the validity and preciseness necessary for upgrading the teaching skills of both the pre-service and the in-service teacher.

The Triple T and similar programs presage a much closer working relationship between universities and public schools for a sounder training of new teachers. Intern programs may move toward an endless variety of work-study formats at different points in the four- or five-year preparation of the professional educator. The single stereotype of the general classroom teacher may very quickly give way to a full playbill of roles, from master teachers with a variety of diagnostic and treatment skills to paraprofessionals with management and clerical skills. Again, it appears to be a case of the formality of past procedures having outlived their usefulness in terms of the changing circumstances of our day. Or perhaps it is a matter of old inefficiencies being starkly revealed and discredited in the light of today's demand for accountability of education from top to bottom.

Applying research technology and inventiveness to local production

As local production of instructional materials continues, we will need to apply more sophisticated approaches and increased expertise in several fields. If not, the homemade item will be much more costly than the value received, particularly when compared to available commercial versions.

Citation Thirty: Each point along the IPC systems flow chart as described in Chapter Two will require upgraded concepts and skills. For example, the relatively precise skill of writing cognitive objectives will have to be duplicated in the formulation of affective objectives. Both lay and professional educational leaders are assigning a much higher priority these days to the achievement of desirable attitudes and values to guide the proper use of improved cognitive skills.

Citation Thirty-one: Preliminary involvement of learners will need to be arranged both to check out the appropriateness of the objectives and to confirm the effectiveness of possible strategies to achieve those objectives. Measuring the effectiveness of various strategies with different students is a very complicated, lengthy task. Curriculum people, with the aid of teachers and research specialists, will have to find practical ways of securing this kind of feedback for confirming or correcting instructional planning while it is still in the process of development.

Citation Thirty-two: One of the first items to be requested for the AV department will be a multiple cassette tape duplicator, if possible one that will reproduce a dual track of sound and automatic advance signals for synchronized slides or filmstrip. Such equipment will be needed as teachers and librarians want to set up many individual learning stations demanding duplicate sets of many audio-visual kits. Even with further refinement of dial-access systems, I do not believe such systems will be as practical as multiple "wet" carrels with "shelf-ready" materials. In the latter case students and teachers can easily maintain control over the selection and use of materials going into the system so as to provide authentic individualization. The former system is still too cumbersome and remote to achieve the same result with similar ease.

Citation Thirty-three: We must organize more effective techniques for revising materials, including specific, valid evidence of what needs to be changed. One- and two-man teams usually rely almost exclusively on their own opinion of what needs to be changed. A research design should be devised which would collect evidence of the impact of the materials when used in different ways with different ability levels. Such research would help pinpoint where alternative strategies and materials are needed to spread success to all types of students. One of the main criticisms of both local and commercial prepackaged curriculums is that they do not provide sufficient variety of activities.

Harnessing technology to carry the repetitious, mundane chores of education

Citation Thirty-four: One product of the new educational-industrial complex is the comprehensive packaged curriculum. These packages contain both benefits and risks.

One element that inflates the risk for businesses involved in such an enterprise is the large initial cost for the design and production of the audio-visual and three-dimensional materials accompanying the more traditional printed materials. An even greater inflation of the risk is due to the fact that the detailed specifications behind the contents of the packages are based on just one small group's assumptions about the nature of the learner, the conceptual structure of a given discipline, and the expectations of society regarding the need for youngsters to understand the concepts and skills of that particular discipline.

The new task of the local curriculum planner is to make a careful analysis† of the available curriculum packages to see how nearly the basic assumptions of the package designers coincide with the basic assumptions of the local staff. This simply stated task of assumption-matching can become very complicated in the execution. One reason for this is that all package designers do not give you an explicit statement of their assumptions. When this is the case, the assumptions have to be inferred from an analysis of the program's objectives and activities.

Another factor that can make the assumption-matching task difficult is the absence of clarity on the part of the local staff about its assumptions regarding the nature of the learner, the structure of the discipline, and the expectations of the community regarding the mastery of a particular discipline by its young. In the case of our revised social studies program described in Chapter Four,

---

† See Appendix A for copy of Ladue's "Design for Unit-Analysis."

it took about three years of deliberations and interactions between the steering committee and the staff to determine the assumptions acceptable at least to the leadership, with the opinion of the total staff still divided. Nevertheless, now, with a generally accepted new rationale and conceptual framework for social studies, all staff members are in a good position to analyze available commercial packages and to quickly determine whether they would be usable alternatives for some of our locally produced units.

As we face an increasing variety of prepackaged curriculums, we need economical ways to make a user's test of the new techniques and materials. A cooperative testing of packages and sharing of field test information among neighboring districts would seem to be a promising approach. Another would be the creation of a regional learning center, which would have all packages on exhibit for interested teachers to test on themselves or on a few youngsters they might have in tow. One point in favor of the center would be that potential users could make a direct comparison of several available alternatives designed for use in the same learning task. The beginnings of such a center have been launched in St. Louis, but its future depends on the support of educational institutions and community agencies of the area.

Citation Thirty-Five: Our district had to make a feasibility study of hardware and software for an in-house teleprocessing computer system. A few years back our high school mathematics department installed a computer terminal to be used in a problem solving mode by advanced students. The device was a great motivator of student interest and a valuable teaching aid for making visible to students each and every mathematical step involved in solving common arithmetic and algebraic problems. It also gave them a new appreciation of the preciseness of mathematical and computer language.

At the same time unit record equipment had been installed in the business office for handling the financial records, payments to venders, and to staff personnel. Report cards, test records, accumulative course records, and address labels were also printed on that equipment.

In two years the mathematics department made increased demands on the computer terminal such that costs for the service were doubled. During the same period, additional jobs were programmed for the unit record equipment, until the system began to reach its capacity in terms of how much could be done in the available time. One possibility was to add speedier components to the unit record installation to take care of the immediate increased demands. A longer look into the future suggested that perhaps the appropriate computer installation would provide all services needed by the business office and at the same time put a computer terminal at the unlimited disposal of math students.

Given the above situation, the Superintendent proposed that the Assistant Business Manager and the Coordinator of Instruction make a feasibility study of a computer configuration which would handle the administrative, business, and instructional needs of our district for the next five years.

After consultation with the appropriate staff and after study of reports of what was being done by other schools, the assistant manager and I drew up a prospectus for the projected utilization of a computer in our district. We listed (1) objectives being accomplished with our present equipment, (2) additional objectives to be accomplished by converting to our own in-house teleprocessing computer system, and (3) long-range objectives that would be made possible by specific expansions and upgrading of the initial computer installation.

Associated with this listing of objectives was a correlated statement of major specifications of storage capacities, modes of input and output, processing speed, mechanical and electronic modes for processing and storage of data, program languages, available peripheral units including teleprocessing connectors, upward compatibility or modular expandibility for future growth, libraries of programs, and company *support services* for installation which included (a) procedures for conversion to new system, (b) adaptations and/or development of programs, (c) the training of operators, and (d) the availability of backup systems. Our final decision on a Honeywell 115 computer was made primarily because of the local support services the company would guarantee at reasonable rates.

At one point in our study the chairman of the mathematics department accompanied the Assistant Business Manager and me on a four-day on-site investigation of computer installations in selected educational institutions in Pennsylvania, Delaware, Ohio, and Kentucky. It was that trip, more than anything else, which convinced us that it would be uneconomical for a district of our size to install one computer capable of integrating all of the administrative, business, and instructional functions that we had projected for the next five years. Rather, we concluded that a total monthly rental of about $3,000 would provide us with our own computer to perform all administrative and business functions, plus two on-line terminals to a computer utility to service our instructional needs at the high school. Our most thoughtful projection of instructional utilization of computers consistently indicated that small specialized stand-alone systems would satisfy our expanded demands most economically for some time, the "switch over" point occurring when we needed more than four student terminals. A great variety of such specialized systems are being proliferated by the very competitive computer industries.

Any investigation of new *hardware* requires an equally serious study of available *software*. In the case of our study of computers, software for administrative and business programs was well developed. However, the programmed material for CAI was available only from a few research centers in universities such as Stanford, Illinois, or Pittsburg, or from the instructional divisions of big city school systems like Philadelphia. Some simulation games leased by private companies were the only additional forms of CAI software turned up by our search. Any general instructional use of computers other than for problem solving seemed a long way off.

The high school business department was interested in an introductory course on business information and data processing. Since the installation of our central office computer, the above course has been launched and classes have come to the computer center for demonstrations. When an advanced course is offered, students will develop simple programs and run them at the center.

We discussed computer data processing with our librarians and found that they gave top priority to the efficient processing of the purchasing of materials. They considered themselves too small an operation to justify book processing and cataloging by computer. However, they had a common interest with us in a related technology, namely, microfilming.

The future developments and applications of microfilming bear watching because of the improved support systems they may provide for curriculum and instruction. Ultramicrofiche, developed by the National Cash Register Company, is already capable of carrying 3,200 pages per card. A 20,000 volume library will fit into thirty-two small card trays. Compact research libraries of unusual depth for teachers and students could be made available in every secondary school. Viewing and printout equipment by DuKane, the Technicolor Corporation, and others will deliver varied services to readers. IBM and other computer manufacturers are developing complex computer installations which electronically store immense libraries, all indexed and accessible for quick retrieval, viewing, and printout. Banks of information equivalent to the Library of Congress may be available to anyone installing the appropriate terminal and paying a rather modest fee.

The video cassette used for storing books to be played in a Motorola EVR and displayed on TV sets at school, home, the library, or any desired place will provide another advanced mode of library service, both audio-visual and portable. The rapidly expanding use of cassette audio tapes presages what may happen in the case of video cassettes. Instructional leaders will need to keep informed of the frontier developments, to be able to anticipate better which information system has the most potential for meeting the school's needs and the least chance of abrupt obsolescence.

Launching the portable VTR

Some of the disappointment over the utilization of instructional television is being balanced by the classroom teacher's use of portable videotape recording systems. As mentioned in Chapter Four, as early as 1966 we successfully used video tape recordings of pilot social studies classes to disseminate new second and fourth grade social studies units throughout our district. This type of use of the portable VTR continues as a part of the on-going in-service in some of our schools.

Drama, speech, English, and social studies departments in our secondary schools make periodic use of the system to record student speeches and dramatic performances for purposes of immediate playback and critique. In-service and pre-service teachers, at their request, may borrow the equipment for self-evaluation of their teaching. The addition of the video-cassettes will make the system even easier for use by both teachers and students. It works best if one staff member in a building becomes the VTR expert and assumes the major responsibility for maintaining the equipment and for giving proper training to all operators. This kind of equipment is subject to all sorts of breakdowns if used indiscriminately by many poorly trained operators. One of our happy discoveries this year is that fifth and sixth grade students can easily be trained to be excellent VTR operators.

VTR systems will become more portable and more operator-proof in the near future. A four-inch video cassette tape will dramatically decrease cost and handling problems. Slow motion recording speeds, single frame displays, and special effects split screens will lead to a limitless variety of beneficial uses.

Half-inch video tape machines have recently been standardized to permit the free exchange of tapes. Companies tell us that it will probably take a couple of years to accomplish the same kind of standardization for video cassette systems. The lack of standardization greatly complicates the problems of the consumer. We presently have four VTRs in our school district, only two of which can exchange tapes. Experience is slowly teaching us that *portability* and *standardization* are criteria equal in importance to high quality output when it comes to the purchase of any kind of audio-visual equipment.

Conclusion

From the very beginning of this book we have talked about curriculum as the never-ending invention of learning environments. We have asserted that persons directly engaged with students, including the students themselves, have the final say about what that curriculum shall be.

Anyone outside the instructional arena of the teacher and the students can influence the character of the curriculum only by altering the inventiveness of the teachers and students and/or by altering the conditions under which their inventiveness is to operate.

The majority of school systems today have large bodies of central office personnel, building principals and interested lay persons (including parents) who want to either support or subvert the curriculum being experienced by the youth.

The message of this book has equal value for the friend or foe of education.

Disparage the style and restrict the resources of a creative teacher and he will become an innocuous, roll-taking order-keeper most pleasing in the eye of the incrustated establishment. Facilitate the style and replenish the resources of a creative teacher and he will become a master inventor of learning environments which refine the skills, expand the concepts and humanize the attitude of all who dwell therein.

As pointed out in the beginning of this final chapter, the ultimate question is: Who shall be disparaged and who facilitated? This judgment is made by the lay and professional leadership of a school district based upon the ends they have chosen for the educational process. From community to community those ends will range *from* the abject shaping of the will and performance of the young for perpetuating the values and position of the status quo *to* the open cultivation of the unique humanity of each person to create an enriched quality of life in future generations.

Given a community which sees education as enabling youngsters to deal with the future rather than perpetuate the past, the curriculum changer still has an enormous task to perform. The remote change agent must upgrade the inventiveness of the classroom curriculum maker and must restructure the institution so that it can embody the new curriculums that are made.

By way of suggesting what the future curriculum worker will need, Joyce has written, "We need to develop laboratories in institutional development." He then proceeds to project a national network of operations that might be such a laboratory for the curriculum worker.

The modest proposal of this book, I believe, is that given the leadership styles and working conditions herein described, the local school district *might* serve as the hub of a laboratory in institutional development. For what would be happening in such a situation would be a very successful extension of what I have described as curriculum renewal, a process involving the restructuring of the social systems of the school as part and parcel with the never-ending invention of more appropriate learning environments for the young.

Design for
unit-analysis

1. *DESCRIPTIVE CHARACTERISTICS*

   What materials are required and how much time is required to teach the unit? Describe all teacher and learner materials, worksheets, equipment, and other physical features or characteristics of the unit including accessibility of these materials to teacher and learner, and approximate length of unit.

2. *CONTENT*

   What information is used to accomplish the objectives? Describe the basic knowledge, concepts, principles or theories, and sources of content. Also describe the maximum depth of content required of the learner.

3. *RATIONALE*

   Why was this particular topic chosen to be taught at this particular time, and why is it important to the learner? Describe the purposes or reasons which are stated or implied in the unit which tend to support it's own existence.

4. *OBJECTIVES*

   What does the learner do during the unit and what can the learner do after studying this unit that he probably could not do previously? Describe the objectives which are stated or implied in the unit, and summarize the objectives in terms of what the learner will be doing related to cognitive and affective skills.

5. *TEACHING STRATEGIES*

   What instructional methods are used to reach the objectives? Describe which teaching strategies are used and to what degree they are emphasized throughout the unit.

6. *EVALUATION CRITERIA*

How will the teacher know the objectives have been reached? Describe the evaluation criteria, test situations, or teacher observations used to measure the outcome of the objectives.

7. *ANTECEDENT CONDITIONS*

What prior skills or knowledge must the learner and the teacher possess to succeed in reaching the objectives? Describe the knowledge and understanding needed for both the learner and the teacher as a necessary prerequisite for success in the unit. Also describe quality of readiness necessary for teacher and learner.

The "Design for Unit-Analysis" is an objective description of a unit of curriculum. There is no attempt to evaluate or make value judgments about the quality of the material at this phase of curriculum investigation. The purpose of a unit-analysis is to quickly and effectively condense an entire unit into a few comprehensive paragraphs in order to aid the teacher or curriculum planner in his next step of unit-evaluation. The unit-analysis provides a capsule view of the entire unit and begins to suggest to the teacher ideas for improving, implementing, or modifying the unit so it will better meet the needs of each classroom situation.

Sample of 3-week unipac in social studies

As a concrete illustration of what confronts the student enrolled in "Innovation 68," I have included a copy of a 3-week Unipac out of the fourth quarter of Social Studies I. It is typical of the kind of packaging that has been done for all courses offered in "innovation" classes.

FOURTH QUARTER
SOCIAL STUDIES I   (INSTRUCTOR'S NAME)

Package XIII—Race relations in Brazil—(three weeks)

Read this entire package before you begin work.

I. *Purpose:*

Racial conflict is a phenomenon that occurs frequently in human history. You have studied its occurrence and the course it has taken in South Africa. In this unit, you will get an opportunity to study the race problem in Brazil and to compare and contrast the Brazilian situation with that in America. Since this is an important problem in our country, we can arrive at a better understanding of it by seeing how it fits into the world picture, and by learning techniques for studying such social problems.

II *Goals:*

Given assigned readings and visuals from both primary and

213

secondary sources about race relations in Brazil, you will analyze these in order to accomplish the following:

A. Determine the frames of reference of the various authors and estimate how their frames of reference affect the usefulness of the evidence.

B. Use the analytical questions which scholars use in political science, economics, and sociology to examine these readings and develop hypotheses with supporting evidence about the following things:

  1. After reading materials about the Portugese, Indians, and Africans, the student will develop a hypothesis predicting what will take place when these races come into contact.

  2. After further readings about the relationship between these groups, the student will modify his hypothesis in the light of the new evidence.

  3. After reading materials about the development of the race problem in the U.S. and in Brazil, the student will be able to compare and contrast the two situations.

  4. After reading primary and secondary sources about today's situation the student will develop a hypothesis and answer this question: How important is a person's race in determining his social position in Brazil today?

  5. Finally, you will arrive at a prediction of your own, based on all of the materials in the unit, about the probable future development of race relations in Brazil.

III. *Activities:*

A. Attend three large group lectures, as follows:

  1. The slave trade—its effect on race relations in North and South America.

  2. History of the development of racial attitudes in the United States: A comparison with Brazil.

  3. To be determined.

B. Read the unit on Race Relations in Brazil in *Non-Western Studies.* You may omit readings VI, XII, and XV.

C. Read Frances Ann Kemble, *Journal of a Residence on a Georgia Plantation* (New York: 1863)—pp. 30–33, 189–191 (enclosed).

D. Attend six seminars, as follows:
1. Background and basic problem. As preparation, complete readings I and II. Take notes and prepare for discussion which will center around goal B–1.
2. The Portuguese and the Indian. Complete readings III and IV, take notes, and prepare for discussion to center on goal #B–2.
3. The Portuguese and the African: Complete readings V and VII and the reading from Kemble (activity "C"). Take notes and prepare for discussion related to goals B–1, B–2, and B–3.
4. The Brazilian Social Structure today: Complete readings VIII, IX, and X. Take notes and prepare for discussion related to goal B–4.
5. Brazilian social attitudes today: Complete readings XI and XIII. Take notes and prepare for further discussion to accomplish goal B–4.
6. Where is Brazil going? Complete readings XIV and XVI. Take notes and prepare for discussion to complete goal B–4 and accomplish goal B–5.

IV. *Evaluation:*

A. After completing activities, take a 25-question objective examination in the materials center.
B. Complete one of the following options:
1. Take a 30-minute examination at the materials center, in which you will be allowed to choose one out of two questions which will be given to you. No notes or other materials may be used. This test should be taken at the same time as the objective examination.
2. Arrange with your instructor to complete a depth or a quest option as outlined in sections V and VI.

V. *Depth:*

A. Read a book on race relations as approached from a scholarly point of view, a book on Negro history, or on Brazilian society and culture. Write and submit a critical review, following "Book Review Requirements." Here are a few suggested books. You may be able to find others.

PART V—INSTRUCTIONAL PACKET

Allport, Gordon W., *The Nature of Prejudice*   325.73
Bibby, Cyril, *Race, Prejudice, and Education.*   323.4
Bishop, Elizabeth, *Brazil.*   918.1
Brown, Ina Corrinne, *The Story of the American
    Negro.*   326.9

B. Scan part VII, "Latin American Society" in Ethel Ewing,
Our Widening World, picking out the portions that deal
with Brazil. In the unit activities, locate the questions that
deal with Brazil and select one for a short research project.
Work out the details of this project with your instructor.

C. Research and write a short paper on one of the following
topics. Include footnotes and bibliography.
  1. The effect of Brazilian independence on race relations
in Brazil.
  2. Comparison of race relations in Brazil and other Latin
American countries.

VI. You may complete a quest with the permission of your instructor.

APPENDIX C

Processing cycles for curriculum development in Ladue

This graph was distributed to all staff members during a Pre-Session Week. It reminded all of some important calendars in our curriculum development process.

	Sept.	Oct.	Nov.	Dec.	Jan.	Feb.	Mar.	Apr.	May	June	July	Aug.
TEXTBOOK CHANGES	Committees Established		Study Made			Recom's Approved		Orders Placed				
NEW SEC. COURSES	Proposals Developed and Submitted				Approved and Announced	Final Preparations Made		Possible Summer Project				
SEC. COURSE OUTLINES AND DESCRIPTIONS		Outlines and Descr. Revised			PRINT							
SUMMER PROJECTS			Applications Dev'd and Submitted			Approval		Preliminary Preparation	Development and Production			
BUDGETS			Needs Projected		Budget Reviewed and Approved			Goods and Services Ordered				

Index